The Way of the Quiet Warrior™

Praise for *The Way of the Quiet Warrior*™

I have experienced firsthand the effects of turmoil in my husband Tom's personal life, and I've watched him take his Hero's journey over twenty years, which led to the creation of The Way of the Quiet Warrior™. *His book gives readers the opportunity to see how he has transcended his, and our, pain and loss, and turned it into a proven blueprint for others to discover true purpose and happiness in marriage, business, and life! A must read that is heartfelt, wise, and beautifully written.*

— **Anna Dutta**, Vice President and Co-Founder, KRE-AT™

Tom Dutta's book, The Way of the Quiet Warrior™, *is a heartfelt, insightful, introspective look at the lifelong process of becoming successful in every area of one's life. I am positive that Tom's candid examination of his personal climb will be highly instructive for anyone who is passionate about creating an extraordinary life. If you refuse to settle for average in your life, this book is a must read.*

— **John Terhune**, Esq., CEO, The RTB Group, LLC

Tom's insight into overcoming seemingly insurmountable odds makes this book a must-read for those held back by the negativity of past life events. Tom makes it clear to all readers of his book that we are capable of much more than we think. Dream big and succeed with a Healthful, Purposeful Life!
— **Derek H. Hall**, Founder and CEO, Qivana

Courage: that is what it takes to write such a book, and that is what the reader gains from reading Dutta's powerful story. Courage to transform one's life.
— **Jon McComb**, Veteran Broadcaster, CKNW

Tom's journey to optimal health, drug-free, is incredible. Everyone needs to read this book to discover a way to achieve health and true happiness.
— **Dr. Nigma Talib**, ND

Vulnerable, inviting, and life changing, The Way of the Quiet Warrior™ *speaks loudly with positive insights about how lives can be best lived despite obstacles. Dutta brings credibility and legitimacy to his work and you will discover powerful truths throughout this book. You will find yourself eagerly anticipating each new twist in this inspiring tale, yet confident and hopeful about your own life in the end.*

— **Dr. Taylor Hartman**

Goals, on their own, are not enough. This book explains a broader approach to manifesting true purpose.

— **Dr. Nancy MacKay**, PhD, CEO, MacKay, CEO, Forums

A heartfelt leadership parable for anyone who has won the world and lost their soul along the way.

— **Jon LoDuca**, Founder and CEO, The Wisdom Link

A story of personal triumph with a map to empower readers to do the same. A great example and lesson for anyone wishing to improve ...in business and in life.

— **Dan Jansen**, Olympic Gold Medalist, Speed Skating

Through moments of true vulnerability, Dutta shows how we can overcome any obstacle to manifest our dreams and make them a reality.

— **Mike Eruzione**, Captain, US Gold Olympic Team, 1980 Miracle on Ice

Tom's book The Way of the Quiet Warrior™ *illustrates the power of personal intention & purpose... interestingly illuminated through multiple metaphors.*

— **Ryan Walter**, Stanley Cup Champion, 17-Year NHL Player & Coach, Leadership/Performance Development Expert

In the pages of this powerful book, you'll discover your hero within.

— **Baraladai Daniel Igali**, Olympic Gold Medalist, Canadian Freestyle Wrestler

A personal exploration of the jagged edges of circumstance and motivation in the quest for a more meaningful life. Dutta's genuine stories will resonate with any individual seeking clarity, hope, and a sincere desire to live a life of meaning and joy.

— **Dr. Salvador Ferreras**, Provost and Vice President, Academic, Kwantlen Polytechnic University

Engaging read and the perfect blend of story telling and practical applications for success that will move you to take action in your life.

— **Maxine Friend**, Psychic and Spiritual Diplomat

By unveiling his own story, Dutta shows how readers can overturn their negative experiences into the very fuel that will ignite a life of higher meaning and purpose.

— **Kamal Dhillon**, Speaker, Advocate, and Author of *Black and Blue Sari*

Most of us work our way through life's challenges blindly. The Way of the Quiet Warrior™ *provides us with a unique perspective on overcoming these challenges on the road to success.*

— **Michael McKnight**, President and CEO, United Way of the Lower Mainland

This book unleashes the power of understanding past life events and future leadership through the experiences of a prominent Canadian leader.

— **The Honourable Mobina Jaffer, Q.C.**, Senate of Canada

The Way of the Quiet Warrior™ *takes us on a journey into the experiences that forge who we become. In this great book, Tom Dutta openly shares his story of high success followed by the series of defeats that allowed him to discover what mattered most. The book gives the reader a very clear and specific way to identify what's been driving them and a system to turn challenges into tools of empowerment. The powerful stories within this book guide the reader to see the value and importance of discovering their own true purpose and offers a system for doing it. I highly recommend* The Way of the Quiet Warrior™.

— **Dov Baron**, Inc Top 100 Leadership Speaker,
Bestselling Author, Mentor to Leaders

The Way of the Quiet Warrior™ *is an inspiring story told through poignant vignettes paired with actionable advice. These real life struggles will resonate with leaders who try to make a difference in their lives and those they inspire. Tom's reference to the People Code and other business tools to understand human behaviour and how it relates to business globally is remarkable. A must-read for students of business written with real life touch.*

— **Balraj S. Mann**, Chairman, BM Group International

Purpose | Action | Life

the way of the Quiet warrior™

90 days to the life you desire

Tom Dutta

NEW YORK

NASHVILLE MELBOURNE

Purpose - Action - Life
The Way of the Quiet Warrior™
90 Days to the Life You Desire

Published in New York, New York, by Morgan James Publishing. Morgan James and The Entrepreneurial Publisher are trademarks of Morgan James, LLC.
www.MorganJamesPublishing.com

The Morgan James Speakers Group can bring authors to your live event. For more information or to book an event visit The Morgan James Speakers Group at www.TheMorganJamesSpeakersGroup.com.

Shelfie

A **free** eBook edition is available
with the purchase of this print book.

CLEARLY PRINT YOUR NAME ABOVE IN UPPER CASE
Instructions to claim your free eBook edition:
1. Download the Shelfie app for Android or iOS
2. Write your name in **UPPER CASE** above
3. Use the Shelfie app to submit a photo
4. Download your eBook to any device

ISBN 978-1-68350-265-4 paperback
ISBN 978-1-68350-266-1 eBook
ISBN 978-1-68350-267-8 hardcover
Library of Congress Control Number:
2016916255

Cover Design by:
Chris Treccani
www.3dogdesign.net

Interior Design by:
Bonnie Bushman
The Whole Caboodle Graphic Design

In an effort to support local communities, raise awareness and funds, Morgan James Publishing donates a percentage of all book sales for the life of each book to Habitat for Humanity Peninsula and Greater Williamsburg.

Get involved today! Visit
www.MorganJamesBuilds.com

DEDICATION

To my creators: my mother Anitra, a protector and a heroine. And to my Father Ashok, whose demons became gifts from God to help me help others.

To my brothers, Robert and Glen, I hope that in sharing my story I can help to bring peace to the both of you on your journeys.

To my wife and business partner Anna Dutta for twenty years of incredible love and marriage. Your support allowed me to discover my purpose and to create The Way of the Quiet Warrior™.

To my three Children Kalinda, Justin and Daniel, our blended family taught me the importance of familial love and parenthood. And, finally, to "little Tommy" who was almost my son: you left me with your story and allowed me to help countless others.

TABLE OF CONTENTS

Introduction

ON THE FORMAT
OF THIS BOOK

What you are holding in your hands is not a typical how-to guide or self-help book. Though The Way of the Quiet Warrior™ formula can help people become better leaders, better partners, parents and friends, it's more than that. It's not about succeeding at work or strengthening interpersonal relationships—at least, not simply about those things. Instead, it's an all-encompassing way of creating our best possible lives of finding out what truly drives us and reconfiguring everything in our lives to move towards that deep purpose. It is the only such formula I know of that is deeply rooted in the motives of the individuals and that approach allows us to help our clients create a path to unprecedented clarity, happiness and success. This formula is unlike any other and I knew that, in order to describe it fully, I would need a book unlike any other.

I spent over three decades in the corporate world where I achieved incredible success as a C-level executive. Though I was successful materially and financially, the more time I spent in that high-powered world, the more aware I was of a few simple, unavoidable facts.

FACT 1: Many—perhaps even most—people live lives of quiet desperation.

FACT 2: People do not discuss this desperation, this unhappiness because...

FACT 3: Most people believe they are doing everything they can to achieve success and that they are on the pathway to happiness and it simply doesn't make sense to them that their path isn't bringing them that happiness. And the final, most devastating FACT was that I was one of these people, stuck on the unthinking treadmill of life and unable to break away and really seek out my true purpose.

To make that change, I had to go on an incredible eight years-long journey. I had to make a lot of mistakes, fall down and get up countless times before I figured out what it was that I truly wanted. It was from that arduous experience that The Way of the Quiet Warrior™ was born and I knew right away that this was something that people needed. Those people I saw around me in the corporate world and elsewhere who were struggling in silence, they needed a way out, they needed a pathway to happiness and I was now uniquely suited to provide one.

When I was working as a CEO and seeking answers to the questions that plagued me of satisfaction, purpose and happiness, I was always very aware of the myriad of "business books" that were available for men and women in my position. I gobbled them up, looking for any advice or guidance that I could get and I admired those books and the people who wrote them but I still realized that something was missing. There were some very engaging and interesting books on the subject but I noticed that a lot of them were very technical, clinical even. There was an element of the impersonal that made it harder for me to connect with the work.

When it came time to write my book, I knew I would have to do something different.

Above all else, I wanted to connect to my readers. I wanted them to find something familiar in my words and in my stories and one of the best ways I've found to connect with people (both in real life and in writing) is to share personal experiences.

I have spent decades working on this program. In some ways, I've been working on it my whole life. During that time, I've spoken with dozens of people who have inspired me with their grace and their vulnerability. People who have honoured me with their most personal, often painful stories.

Vulnerability, unfortunately, is an under-valued virtue, particularly in the corporate world. Too often, we equate vulnerability with weakness but it is not the same at all. A true willingness to expose our flaws and our fears and our past traumas is an incredible strength and people who are willing and able to do that should be lauded, not derided.

I do recognize, though, that the world doesn't always work that way. After years of working on my own life and moving through all the phases of The Way of the Quiet Warrior™ personally, I have gotten to a place where I'm comfortable talking about all the most challenging parts of my life within these pages. I knew, though, that I couldn't make that decision for the people who had trusted me with their stories over the years.

At the same time, their stories were incredible and provided clear illustrations of why The Way of the Quiet Warrior™ is necessary and how it can make huge changes in people's lives. I wanted to include their voices and experiences in some way because I knew that there were people out in the world who would read those stories and say "yes, that's me. I've been in that place." I am a big fan of Joseph Campbell's concept of "The Hero's Journey" which is a narrative structure that spans cultures and languages and essentially describes the full development of a seemingly ordinary person into a hero. I was attracted to the universality of that journey, which I think also speaks to many events in my life and in the lives of people I have known. The idea that so many people could find relevance in Campbell's ideas, not just in terms of stories but in terms of their own lives speaks to how much we have in common with one another.

Human beings like to imagine that our stories are unique and that we are alone in our suffering but the truth is that no matter what you have experienced, no matter how difficult or painful, there is someone else out there in the world who has been through that exact same thing. We are never alone, not if we are willing to reach out to one another.

I wanted to provide that feeling of connection and validation for my readers. I wanted to show them that they didn't have to try to solve all their problems on their own but they could, instead, embrace a formula that will provide help and guidance as they journey towards the best possible version of their lives.

To that end, I designed the distinctive structure of this book. Inside, you will find six "factual" chapters, describing what you can expect from each of the six phases of The Way of the Quiet Warrior™ and what those phases can do for you. Interspersed with these chapters are fictional stories designed to illustrate the concepts detailed in the phases. These stories are drawn from real life and real people that I have known over the years, both personally and professionally. In many cases, these are events that I was directly involved in and I observed first hand how the The Way of the Quiet Warrior™ principles made real changes in the lives of real people.

I have drawn extensively from my own life and experiences but we are almost never alone in our experiences and, to protect the privacy of these other people and to honour the trust they placed in me, I have fictionalized their life and stories. I've combined characters or added fictionalized elements, I've moved the action to different places or changed circumstances to disguise the actual people involved. The feelings, the challenges and the breakthroughs are all real but the characters are just that: characters and not explicit depictions of anyone.

You might call it the "based on a true story," approach.

My belief is that this unusual structure will serve a few purposes, allowing me to share insights without turning a spotlight on specific people while also engaging the reader in a new way. This is unlike any other "business book" you have read before, just like The Way of the Quiet Warrior™ is a motive-based formula unlike any other.

This book is designed to go hand-in-hand with a constellation of other elements including The Way of the Quiet Warrior™ formula itself and my company KRE-AT™, which offers a wealth of services, including a highly calibrated personal profile and a discovery lab that allows you to explore the formula in a more hands-on way. At the back of this book, you will also find some sample materials that offer an example of the kind of tools that will help you move through the phases of the formula. In particular, there is a unique Self-Assessment Quiz that will lead you to take the "PROFILE" and begin your own journey of discovery!

This book—and The Way of the Quiet Warrior™ formula in general—is a resource. Take it and use it and let your personal adventure begin!

THE BOY

C hew it," his father said, "it'll clean your teeth."

The boy bit down on the small chunk of charcoal and it crumbled easily. It didn't taste like much of anything, like dirt a little and like minerals. He could feel it scraping and grinding against his teeth.

"Spit," his father said and he obeyed, producing a blob of inky saliva. It seemed impossible that this could have made his teeth any cleaner but his father knew many things the boy did not know. Maybe this was one of them.

His father taught him to use a rifle in much the same way, standing back and issuing orders in short, staccato sentences.

"Press it into your shoulder. Tight."

"Squeeze, don't pull."

"Stop shaking."

His father did not move his arm into position or guide his hand against the stock. He was mostly sober when he taught the boy and his brothers how to use the rifle and he didn't touch them much when he was mostly sober.

1

"Don't flinch," he said, when the rifle exploded, filling the air around him with unbearable sound.

The boy had no memory of the island, though his mother had described it to him many times. He liked the sound of it: *Suva*. It rolled on his tongue like a thick dessert.

His mother talked about it more when it was cold, when it was raining, when the old soreness in her back sang and throbbed. She told him how happy they were, how good things were. She told the boy about his father when his hair was smooth and thick and dark, parted with a ruler and a protractor, a perfectly upright, young Mormon man.

"He was so *good*," she would tell him, something apologetic and something grasping in her voice. It was as though she needed something from her son, some forgiveness or some reassurance, or perhaps just a simple understanding that she never meant for things to end up how they did.

The boy never blamed her though; he understood. His father had a . . . quality about him. When he wanted to, he could look at you and make you feel as though you weren't just the only person in the room, but also, the only person *ever*.

Who wouldn't fall in love with that? Everyone loved his father; Army buddies, schoolmates, strangers on the street, women of all types, and, of course, the boy loved his father. Even when he hated him too.

Miss McClelland was the youngest teacher in the elementary school and one of the shortest. When she stood in a crowd of seventh graders, it was hard to tell her apart from the children. She had unusually large blue eyes and tight, reddish-brown curls. The boy was not the only one in the class who loved her but he was pretty sure that he was the only one she loved back.

The boy knew she loved him by her smile when she called on him in class and the way she let him sit out recesses or eat his lunches in the hallway outside her classroom. She never embarrassed him by asking him why he didn't want to play with the other kids, why he preferred to eat alone and unseen. Instead, she gave him the gift of silence. Occasionally, she would walk by and see him sitting with his back against the cold stone wall and give him another one of her melting smiles.

Once, after a group of boys had driven him off the playground with shouts of "Hindu" and "raghead," she had allowed him to seek shelter in her classroom. She chattered brightly, examining her one-shelf library and extolling the virtues of each volume while the boy tried to find something to say.

He could tell her that it wasn't even true, that he wasn't a raghead. He knew because he had looked it up. The first time he heard it—was *called* it—he didn't know what it meant but he could tell that it was bad, so he didn't dare ask his mother. He looked in a dictionary and, apparently, it was a word for someone who was from Arabia. He wasn't from Arabia; he was born in England. He did have a grandmother, his father's mother, who was born in Southeast Asia in a place called Kashmir. She had come visit sometimes, never for very long, and every time, she wore a loose, draping sari and kept her hair in the same long, dark plait. They had no language in common, the boy and the old woman, so she would sit quietly, looking at nothing in particular, and he would go about his business. After a while, he would forget that she was there, like a sofa or a table, and then she would shift slightly, let out the smallest of sighs and the boy would be startled again by her existence.

But Miss McClelland wouldn't care about all that.

"It might be a little advanced," she said, pulling an elderly paperback from the shelf, "but you're smart, aren't you?" She said it with a wink in her voice, like it was a fact already agreed upon, but the boy was not so sure. The most his father had ever said of him was that at least he wasn't "a retard" like his younger brother, with his jittery, uncontrollable exclamations.

The book displayed a picture of a woman with snakes for hair on the cover; *An Encyclopedia of Greek Mythology*, it read.

"Read a little bit every day," Mrs. McClelland told him, "and then come in here for lunch and we'll talk about it." She said it like it was an order or an instruction, rather than a life preserver tossed to him out of simple kindness, and maybe a bit of pity.

The boy just nodded, he didn't trust his voice enough to thank her. Would he sound small or pathetic or weak or any of the other things he secretly suspected himself to be? He couldn't bear to have *her* of all people think of him like that. Instead, he smiled as hard as he could.

His mother was the stalwart canary in the coal mine of their home. The boy looked to her first thing before he did anything else because he could tell by the expression on her face, by the way she held herself, how bad it was going to be.

If she seemed stiff, her face remote and tight as though she were struggling to hold a very heavy weight without complaining, then the boy knew that his father was still in the slow ramping-up process. Maybe he was still only drinking and giving his family long, blistering looks full of loathing. Maybe he was out, in parts unknown with folks unknown. Either way, the pressure was still building and the man had not yet exploded.

It was almost better, those days when she was teary-eyed and cowering, because it meant that the storm had broken. Instead of tight and stiff, her body would sag with a kind of terrible relief. The boy's father might be hitting the walls or hitting the four of them but at least it was happening outright, no more waiting or imagining or anticipating. Soon enough, he would exhaust himself or saturate himself with booze and fall into that deathlike sleep and, for a little while, they'd have silence.

The worst thing was when the boy came home and found that his mother was not there at all. She wasn't in the kitchen preparing an after-school snack or in the living room tidying. Instead, he would find her shut up in his parents' darkened bedroom, lying in the same position in which he'd left her that morning when he went to school.

She wasn't sleeping. There was a thin crack where the curtains didn't quite cover the windows and he could see how the light caught on her open eyes, giving them a gleam.

"Are you hurting?" he asked, touching the back of his hand to her forehead, because that was what she did for him when he was sick. Her skin was cool and dry but she nodded all the same.

This sadness was an old wound, like the one in her back. When conditions were just right, it flared into life and kept her confined to her bed. Once, when the boy was very small, it got so bad that she had to go away for a long time, several weeks. The boy and his brother were not allowed to visit her and, when she came back, she looked somehow smaller than they'd remembered.

The boy wanted to ask her to promise him that she wouldn't go away again but he had a feeling that would upset her and his father was there, watching the reunion with the same evaluating eye he had when teaching the children how to shoot or cut wood or change a tire or any of the other things that made a man a man.

His father had told the both of them once that they were lucky to have a mother like her, a mother who cared for them and looked out for them.

"Not everyone has that," he'd told them. He never seemed to remember those sentiments when he was calling her stupid, ugly, or useless.

"When your father was young . . ." Their mother spoke of him as a young man so delicately, so differently. It was like she was talking about another person altogether, someone who had perhaps died young and tragically. ". . . he had a hard time. His mother did some things that he . . . finds hard to forgive." She wouldn't look at the boys when she said that part.

The boy wasn't sure exactly what she meant—he would not know for many years, not until he was a man himself—but he did recall watching his father once when his grandmother was visiting. The old woman was silent with her son as well; though they might have spoken, neither did. Once, though, she had reached out to him over the kitchen table. She'd reached out as if to cover his hands with her own and the boy had watched his father flinch away from her touch like it was a burning ember.

"My little Elvis," the boy's mother called him, smoothing back his dark hair, "my little man."

Sometimes, she would hold his face in both her hands and just look at him, with the fondest expression on her face. The boy bloomed under her gaze. He wanted to be everything she thought he was, everything she needed him to be.

And so he checked in, every day, to read her face and look for the signs and, if necessary, prepare. His father channeled his rage into the most readily available target but he did have his preferences. The eldest brother was off-limits, the first-born son and a father's prize, he alone was treated as precious, at least physically. The boy's little brother was too sprightly, a ham and an entertainer who tried to distract their father by fooling around and making him laugh. He was no good to hurt. Their mother was too passive; she absorbed the stream of harsh words like a kitchen sponge. Sometimes that only seemed to make the boy's father angrier.

"Why do you just sit there?" he would yell. Sometimes he would throw things at her, just to see her move.

The boy was in between, Goldilocks's perfect porridge. He wasn't clever enough to make jokes or confident enough to perform and he couldn't sink into himself the way his mother could. Every blow, every word, it all showed on him and his father liked that. The boy supposed that everyone likes to see that their work is doing something, changing something in the world, even if it is just a little boy's expression or the skin on his arms, his chest, his throat.

"Your father's having people over," she told him when he got home from school. She was scrubbing dark scratches out of the surface of the sink, one elbow crooked, the motion of her hand, fast and violent.

The boy nodded and went to his room and fell asleep. That was the best time to sleep, if he could manage it. There would be noise when his father came back, even if he came alone, and the boy could never completely rest when he knew his father would soon be arriving. His stomach would wake him, a stab like hunger pangs and a nausea so intense that his mouth filled with sickly saliva.

Now, though, the house was empty and they were all fortifying themselves, the same way someone might board up the windows and fill a bathtub with water when a hurricane was inbound. His mother would scrub and polish their already immaculate home. The boy would sleep as deeply as he could manage, ready to be available but unobtrusive the moment that his father appeared on the doorstep.

His mother didn't like the parties, never had. She usually tried to vanish into some secluded part of the house and, if it was a good night, the boy's father would let her.

The boy tried to sleep like he always did, curled tightly in on himself with the blanket wrapped around his face, leaving just the smallest hole for breathing, but there was something restless in him. He kept thinking about the book Miss McClelland had given him—and about Miss McClelland herself.

Eventually, he tossed the covers off, retrieved the book from his backpack, opened it to the first chapter: *Cronus Devouring His Children,* and started to read.

The boy's father was very good at parties. He could smile so widely and so brightly and laugh so heartily and look at people so earnestly that they didn't want to do anything other than sit in the tractor-beam of his gaze.

He had party tricks, but they were all at the expense of someone else. One of his favorites was to grab the boy while he was on his way somewhere else and pull him into a little semicircle of adults. Sometimes the boy knew them, neighbors or men his father worked with; some were strangers, giving him the same dreamy, indulgent stare of someone who is seeing the world through a vodka-soft filter.

"Look at this," his father would say, lifting up his son's shirt. "Look at this!" he would say again and laugh, grabbing a bit of the boy's belly in his hand and shaking it to gales of laughter. Then, his father would shake his head and shrug as if to say, *Isn't it crazy how* that *came from* me? and everyone would laugh again because it really was crazy.

Cronus was a titan, one of the most powerful beings on Earth, yet there was a power still greater: that of his own father, Uranus. In a plot with his mother, Gaia, and his monstrous siblings, Cronus usurped his father and dismembered him, scattering his parts into the endless sea where they became the basis for the nations of the Earth we know.

His triumph was tempered, however, by the knowledge that just as he had betrayed and destroyed his father, so too was Cronus destined to be overthrown by his own children. Five children he produced, five gods and goddesses of unimaginable power and he consumed each one of them the moment they were born to forestall the prophecy of his own destruction.

But the sixth child—and the youngest—was called Zeus and he was too beloved by his long-suffering mother. She refused to give him up to be devoured and, instead, substituted a large stone in swaddling clothes. Cronus, none the wiser, ate the stone and never realized that his promised doom, his only living son, was growing into manhood right under his nose.

The boy's father tried to teach him, once or twice, about women. About how to look at them, about how to tell a good one from a bad one.

"That one," he would say, pointing to a slim young woman in a long, dark skirt, "that is a good one for a wife." Others he would single out as "for fun." There was no commonality to these women. Some were short; some were tall. Some were plump; some were thin. They had black hair and red, gleaming brown skin and splashes of freckles. They wore shorts and dresses and long raincoats. They had children of their own or were clearly still in high school. "Slut," he would say, almost with approval.

There were far fewer wives than there were sluts, the boy learned.

Sometimes, the boy looked at the old pictures his mother kept from her earliest courtship. His father, in a short-sleeved button-down shirt and his mother, beside him, small and beaming. Her hair was longer than, dark bird-wings swooping away from her face and she seemed to stand a little taller. Of course, her back had not hurt her so much back then. The boy looked at her face and tried to see the thing in it that had convinced his father that she wasn't just *a* wife but *the* wife, the only one for him. As much as he tried, though, he could see nothing that would set her apart from the other women, from the sluts.

One day, the boy came home from school to find his mother sitting at the kitchen table with the phone held limply in her hand. He could hear the dull, regular beeping coming from the upturned plastic and the cord was twisted around her arm like an ugly bracelet. She wasn't looking at anything, just staring the same way she did when she went to her bed but he had never seen her look that way before when she was sitting up.

The boy took the phone from her hand. Delicately, he untangled the cord and it was like changing a sleepy baby. Her limbs were heavy and her movements dreamlike, she allowed her son to move her arms around at will until he had settled both her and the receiver back where they belonged.

"What should I do?" she asked him, her voice very small, smaller even than the boy's. "What should I do?"

She couldn't tell him then, though she would some days later, about how she had received a call from a little girl no older than the boy's little brother. The child had called to complain about the strange man who came over to her house all the time, who locked the little girl outside while he visited with her mother for hours on end.

"I don't like him," the little girl had said. "I don't want him to come around no more."

"He said he wouldn't," the boy's mother told him. "He said he wouldn't do it ever again." He had probably meant it too, the boy thought. His father was always so genuinely sorry; it was just that he always seemed to forget. Like childbirth or a youthful injury, his contrition was a pain that always faded and he had to remind himself of the feeling.

Zeus grew, raised by nymphs on a steady diet of milk and honey and far from his father's roving eye. When he had come into the fullness of his manhood, he began to feel the weight of responsibility, the pull to complete his destiny and end his own father.

To do that, he had to take back what should have been his; he had to free his siblings from their father's awful gullet. Some stories say that a crafty Gaia, mother of Cronus, slipped her son a poisonous herb that made him vomit everything he contained. Other stories say that it was Zeus himself who sliced his father open, perhaps using the same scythe that Cronus had used to dispatch his own father.

Either way, the five glorious siblings of Zeus emerged from the wreckage of their father's flesh and, together, they imprisoned the remaining titans in the land of the unquiet dead, Tartarus. The six gods of the new world then drew lots to determine their dominion. For Zeus, who was to be king of the gods, there was the realm of air and sky. They would call him the lightening god and, when the sky shook, the people would say that he was angry.

"Look at you," the woman on the sofa cooed, her words half formed and almost dripping out of her mouth. "A regular little maid."

The boy picked up an overflowing ashtray on the coffee table in front of the woman and a half-empty beer bottle from the floor next to her foot. He liked to keep on top of the mess as it was being created; it was all so much easier that way.

This was a good party. It was nearly 2:00 a.m. and there had been no fighting, no yelling, nothing broken and only some minor stains. Once, his father had put his hand through the glass patio door and just stood there, marveling at the blood that flickered over his hand and arm like Christmas ribbon. Tonight, there had been no blood.

The boy's little brother was asleep on the other side of the sofa, exhausted from his court-jester duties. The boy covered him in an afghan and, occasionally, the drunk woman would lean over and smooth his hair.

"You Arabs make such pretty babies," she mused and the boy did not bother to correct her. She was the wife of their two-doors-down neighbor. The boy went to school with her daughter, a quiet, blonde-haired girl who sometimes gave him sympathetic looks when the others were taunting him.

The boy carried the ashtray into the kitchen and dumped its contents into the trash, pausing at the sink to empty the rest of the beer. The woman on the sofa and her husband were some of the few remaining guests. Most had stumbled homeward and one was sleeping soundly in the spare bedroom. The boy figured that he could go to bed now, secure in the knowledge that the party was burning down to glowing coals. No one would be hurt now; nothing would be destroyed. Tomorrow was Saturday and his father would be hungover. Maybe all of them could sleep in.

He found them in the hallway just outside his own bedroom. His father, towering unsteadily over the smaller figure, dipped his head and said something that made her laugh, though it sounded a little nervous. The boy could see the outline of her wild curls and, as he watched, his father raised his hand and tangled his fingers in them.

Miss McClelland stood there, a paper cup in her hand. She was wearing a dress the boy had never seen her wear before. She had her back against the wall and, as the boy watched, his father half leaned, half crashed into her, pressing his face against her ear and neck.

The boy felt hot and cold at the same time. It was like touching the metal part of an iron: the temperature was too extreme to identify, all he knew was that it hurt.

―――――――

His mother was not asleep. She was not in her bed at all; instead, there was just a pile of discarded coats and bags. The boy wondered briefly if one of them belonged to Miss McClelland. He almost wanted to find it and take something from it, take something from her. He wanted to hurt her, even if it was just in the tiniest of ways.

The bathroom door was shut and when the boy knocked, he heard his mother call out in a trembling voice, "I'm almost done."

"It's me," he said and, after a moment, she pushed the door open. She was sitting on the closed toilet, still fully clothed with even her socks on. Her eyes were big and her knees were trembling slightly.

The boy did not say anything but only launched himself into her arms. She held him without question or comment, rocking him gently like he was a little baby instead of almost twelve years old.

"I hate parties," the boy muttered into her shoulder.

"Me too," his mother whispered.

One day, many years in the future, his mother would tell him about another party of sorts, one that happened before she and his father got married. He had returned from the military base where he was stationed with a group of men. "Hungry men!" he'd shouted, jovially drunk. He wanted—demanded—a meal and she had struggled to make one but they had little in the house in the way of food and certainly not enough for the small battalion he had brought home.

He had flipped, as he did so often and so easily, from cheerfully sauced to wrathful, accusing her of defying him, sassing him back, being a bad wife, and undercutting him as a man. In a moment of rage, he had half shoved, half thrown her into the empty fireplace in their little house.

He broke her back, broke her in half, left her with a constant pain that dogged her for the rest of her life. He broke her against the stones of the hearth and left her there, sobbing and scared, half certain that she was going to be paralyzed.

The boy did not ask her why, why she hadn't immediately left as soon as she had healed but he didn't have to ask. It was in his eyes and it was in her heart, all the time.

"He was so sorry," she said. "He got on his knees for me. He told me that he would never hurt me again, that he would take care of me for the rest of my life." She hesitated slightly and then added: "And I had you, you and your brother, not even two years old."

Zeus was a powerful god, though not always a good or reasonable one. He was capricious and angry, licentious and deceitful. He rained down punishment for the most minor of offenses and regularly broke his vows to his sister-consort and to others.

What he did not do, however, was consume his children. He allowed them to be born, to grow, even to have a place at his side, if they so chose. He had learned at least that lesson from his father and his father's father, and he never tried to snuff the life from his progeny out of fear that they would one day destroy him.

And thus they never did.

1 PHASE ONE
THE
SELF

What are your strengths? Limitations?
Why do you do what you do?

Why did you do that?
Why did you say that?
Why are you *like* that?

These are questions that most of us have confronted in our lives. Sometimes they come from employers, friends, or partners. Most often, though, these questions come from deep within ourselves.

Self-help systems and business-efficacy guides are concerned with behavior: stopping negative behaviors, instituting positive behaviors, changing the behaviors of others. What these programs often miss, however, is the critical topic of *motivation*. I believe that no one can truly make meaningful changes to his life and behavior until he delves into his own motivations and the things that drive him.

This is very difficult work for most people. Our motivations are often rooted in deep, almost primordial parts of our psyches and it can be painful to venture into those places that we so often try to ignore. Part of the difference in The Way of the Quiet Warrior™ is a conviction that many of our motivations are inherent or cemented very early in life and tend not to be changed dramatically over the course of our lives. We consider motivations to be an intrinsic part of people and investigating motivations, like investigating any other bedrock of what makes us *ourselves* can be challenging or scary. In my experience, however, it is infinitely more destructive to pretend that dark place doesn't exist.

I say this not just as someone who has developed a system for stopping stagnation and creating personal growth but as someone who has spent years struggling against the darker parts of my nature and my past. The illustrative stories in this book are fictionalized but they are rooted in real people and real situations that I have encountered and, in some cases, that I have lived through.

My father was indeed an alcoholic. A man tortured by his own abusive upbringing, he was by turns a harsh, militaristic taskmaster who demanded the highest level of achievement and a sloppy drunk who passed out on the lawns of strangers (or, on one alarming occasion, in the lobby of a hotel) and made no attempt to hide his many adulterous affairs. He hit me. He belittled me. He made our house a place of constant fear and habitually put the future of our family in jeopardy. He was also my father, the only one that I would ever get, and no matter how unfair it felt, that was my upbringing. I did not have the benefit of a safe and stable home. I did not have caregivers whom I could trust to meet my physical and emotional needs. Instead, I had been dealt a different sort of hand in life and I developed tools that made sense for the life I had.

As I grew into adulthood, however, I slowly began to realize that the ways I had taught myself to navigate situations and relationships were really only effective for toxic relationships like the ones I had with my family. In fact, when I tried to apply my experience and my knowledge to positive relationships or situations, I found that I inevitably ended up destroying them. I didn't have the vocabulary at the time, but now, I would say that I was living within the limitations of my personality instead of playing to my strengths.

During this time in my life, I had a strong narrative about why I did the things I did and why I failed in the specific ways I consistently found myself failing. It all came back to my father. My father was an alcoholic, an abuser; he had done this to me. He had ruined me. He had made my life what it was. In this narrative, my own choices were negligible, already predetermined by the things I had suffered as a child. Years later, Tony Robbins would call this narrative my "bullshit story," my easy excuse for everything that didn't really get at the real issue.

I allowed that narrative to rule me for a long time. I was afraid to really dig into the dark places and find out the *why* behind the things I was doing, and as a direct result of those choices, I lost relationships (including a marriage). I trapped myself in a career that was crippling me with anxiety and depression. And I generally stalled out in my growth as a human being. My story is unique to me and my background is certainly not the only way to wind up stuck in limitations. It's not *just* alcoholism or *just* abuse or *just* the immigrant experience or *just* any one thing. There are, tragically, a million ways that a person can become damaged and get stuck in a cycle of toxic choices. I saw that firsthand with my father.

Many alcoholics never get sober, not for longer than a few months—a few years, at best. Many don't have sufficient incentive to stop drinking, while others don't have a support structure in place or the internal makeup to stay away from the bottle in the long term. Some of them die by disease or by accident, killed by their addiction in one way or another.

When I was younger, I expected that my father would be like that. I couldn't imagine he would ever stop; it was too much a part of him. When my mother told me stories of him as a young man—a teetotaler who wouldn't touch anything stronger than a glass of orange juice—it seemed like she was telling me a fairy tale or a legend about someone who had never really existed. I couldn't picture my father without his addiction; I didn't even know what that man would look like.

I did eventually find out but only after my father had hit the lowest possible point. He lost his wife, his career, any kind of respect he'd had in his community and, during one particularly terrible binge, he very nearly became a murderer, causing an auto accident that almost claimed several innocent lives. On top of all of that, the alcohol was literally killing him, poisoning his body and destroying his health. That was what it took for him to break away and get sober.

His sobriety didn't fix our relationship, of course. His sobriety couldn't erase the pain he'd caused me—every kind of pain a person can experience—but it did crack open the door and allow me to at least see him again. I couldn't connect with my father when he was drinking. Seeing him drunk, even just seeing him in proximity to alcohol, triggered that familiar tightness in my chest, that same apprehension. It turned me into a scared kid, waiting for his dad to get home and hoping desperately that he would pass out instead of come looking for a fight.

It seemed that sobriety did something similar for my father as well. It was only after he had quit drinking that he was able to be truly honest with me. Only when he was sober could he open up to me about his own upbringing, so incredibly similar to my own.

My father was born to Indian immigrants in Fiji. He was raised a Hindu but he gravitated toward the Mormon faith as a young adult. His life was all restriction on one hand and incredible, destructive indulgence on the other. His own father was completely consumed by alcohol, to the point of being nonfunctional when he even brushed up against sobriety. His mother—my grandmother—didn't question or object. She came from a background in which a woman's role in her marriage was very clearly defined: she was to be a helpmeet to her husband. If that meant brewing liquor in her own kitchen because he had drunk away their last penny, that was what she did. My grandfather never hit his lowest point because my grandmother was always crushed beneath him, cushioning the fall. Eventually, his addiction killed him. His body, ravaged by drink, gave out at the family dinner table with my father right there, a horrified witness. I never met my grandfather but, in many ways, I lived with the fallout of his choices.

My father hated his father, hated his addiction, and hated alcohol most of all. Like many children of alcoholics, he vowed that he would never touch the stuff and, like many children of alcoholics, he eventually found that was a promise he could not keep.

My father never reckoned with his childhood, with his parents and all the ways they'd failed him. Instead, he replicated the behaviors he had seen from them and rushed to the same coping mechanisms that had destroyed his family. When my father told me the story of his father's death, I saw him in a new light for the first time. He wasn't an adversary; he wasn't the architect of all my dysfunction. He was a mirror. Or, he would be, if I didn't start making some changes.

That is why the first phase in The Way of the Quiet Warrior™ is called "THE SELF," because no journey of any magnitude takes place without a serious, thorough accounting of your current self. When we start looking at THE SELF, we first have to confront that question: what truly motivates us? I had to look beyond immediate, specific motivations like "a year-end bonus" or "upcoming vacation." I even had to broaden the scope of my search beyond my deeper, more hidden impulses to reenact parts of my difficult childhood. It was only when I really looked at my decisions not as individual moments but as part of a pattern of values and priorities that I really understood what I wanted. Or, better yet, what I *needed*.

What I finally discovered was that I had long been driven by a need for intimacy. Not necessarily romantic intimacy, but a general sense of closeness to the people in my life, whether they were family, friends, or even coworkers. I habitually made choices that I believed would strengthen and intensify the bonds I had with others and I let my feelings about individuals guide me in virtually all aspects of life, even if I didn't realize it at the time.

Much later, I would come to realize that this sort of motivation was part of a suite of personality characteristics that Dr. Taylor Hartman would group together and call "Blue."

To be Blue was to be driven by closeness and depth of relationships, to struggle with anxiety and worry, and to wrestle with a strong tendency toward perfectionism. On the other hand, the natural talents of a Blue personality include "quality" and "service" as well as dependability and sincerity, and when a given personality is playing to his or her strengths—we'd refer to

Kid's Quiz   Contact   Blog   Store

Print Report

Blue

Congratulations Tom Dutta, you are a core **BLUE** personality motivated by your driving core motive **INTIMACY**, with a **RE** secondary color. This report has been specifically customized for you!

YOUR SCORES

BLUE 51%   RED 37%
WHITE 6%   YELLOW 4%

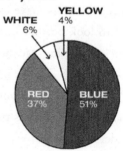

WHITE 6%
YELLOW 4%
RED 37%
BLUE 51%

....Your Personality Style as a BLUE....

As a BLUE, your greatest desire is to love someone and be loved in return. For you,

this situation as a "healthy Blue"—we are capable of incredible things. Each personality type is, in fact, and no one type is any more effective or more wonderful than another, it's all simply a matter of understanding what we are good at and the places where we tend to get stuck.

Dr. Hartman wrote a number of books detailing his study of how people relate to one another and the motives that drive them. I was very drawn to his ideas and was able to apply many of them in my own life. Eventually, we formed a partnership, working together to bring Dr. Hartman's motivation-based systems to people who are feeling trapped or desperate in their current lives. I had discovered in my own life and career that there were any number of vehicles that would allow me to get from one point to another and when I discovered The People Code, I recognized immediately that this was a very effective vehicle that would allow me to teach others the things I'd learned during my own journey.

Dr. Hartman has identified four main "types" of people who were associated with a different primary fundamental motivation and gave each of them a colour: Red, Blue, White, and Yellow. You could call these people by many terms (if we were living in the Middle Ages, for example, we might say someone was "choleric" or "phlegmatic" rather than Red or Blue) but I like Dr. Hartman's assessment and find it generally useful for identifying, broadly speaking, common sets of strengths and limitations that we see recurring together in many people. Blues, like myself, make up about 35 percent of the population, while Reds comprise roughly 25 percent. Superficially, these colours can appear to oppose one another. When we talk about how these personalities work, we often talk about them in terms of how they manipulate or control people, but this is not exactly as Machiavellian as it seems. Most group dynamics in the world hinge upon some members of the group influencing other members to act in certain ways. The Reds and Blues of the world tend to spend their life controlling others with logic and emotion; the Whites and Yellows tend to spend their life trying to avoid being controlled. All personalities have a place in society but, when people indulge in the worst aspects of their character, toxic environments can emerge.

A Red personality type is motivated by power, not being good or bad, but in the sense of getting things done, moving from A to B; this is how they love the world. In the abstract, this can sound negative, even sinister, but that is not necessarily the case. Certainly, there are toxic Red personalities who selfishly use and abuse others in order to meet their goals, but Reds are also confident, assertive, motivated, decisive, and often have a natural talent for vision and leadership. If you are lost in a strange city, you want a Red personality by your side because, within minutes, they will have found the nearest landmark and mapped out a route and they won't stop until the problem is solved. Similarly, a seemingly benign Blue personality can be incredibly destructive if they allow themselves to obsess over perfecting a project to a point of paralysis or overwhelm others with their emotional intensity. When Blues are firing on all cylinders, they can be incredibly loyal, caring, and intuitive leaders, but their flaws can be just as destructive as Reds' flaws, under the right circumstances.

The late Steve Jobs was a classic example of a Red leader, someone with an incredible vision that he was able to realize, but often at the cost of alienating, hurting, or even destroying the people around him. Many Reds are emotionally immature and in Steve Job's case, he struggled to deal with traumas inflicted early in life.

I, myself, have seen all sides of motive-based leadership. I personally have been an effective and a very ineffective Blue-style leader. I have used my impulse toward relationship building to create close-knit teams that were able to achieve incredible things, but I have also overwhelmed people with a need for perfection and anxiety about the future.

When a person gets stuck in his or her worst impulses, we call that "living in your limitations." Each of the personality types has potential trouble spots, places where people can become stuck and wind up acting out the same negative behaviors over and over again. The Way of the Quiet Warrior™ is designed to allow people to clearly see when they are living in their limitations and give them the antidotes to those destructive patterns.

White and Yellow personalities each comprise about 20 percent of the population. People with White personalities are driven by the motive of peace, not in the sense of a cease-fire in a war, but in terms of generalized harmony among the people around them. I often ask folks to imagine their "happy place," perhaps a stream meandering around rocks beneath a sky dotted with fluffy, marshmallow clouds, and that is where a White personality wants to live all the time. They avoid conflict whenever possible and they tend to be somewhat opaque, retreating into themselves in challenging situations.

There are many White types among our diplomats, doctors, and lawyers—jobs that require clarity, reason, and an aptitude for defusing tense situations. My Whites have a natural talent for clarity of thought and they are excellent voices of reason. They are even-tempered and patient, and their natural avoidance of conflict leads them to make peace between warring factions. A White personality at the top of his or her game is exactly what you would want in a caregiver or advocate: kind, patient, empathetic, and an excellent listener. This same type of people, however, can also shut down in the face of a difficult decision or simply because they feel overwhelmed. They can be uncommunicative, especially when they are struggling, and it can be incredibly difficult for outsiders to guess what is going on behind their neutral expression.

Yellow personalities are driven by pure, unadulterated fun. They are joy-seekers, relentless optimists who have great reservoirs of enthusiasm and optimism. A person with a Yellow personality type is always very "present," very in the moment. This makes them very vital and engaging, but it also often means that they are poor long-term planners who can quickly get in over their head in difficult situations. As you might expect of folks driven by the pursuit of fun, Yellow personalities also get bored easily and can be notorious for leaving projects half finished. Staying committed, whether it is to a person, a job, or even a career is a challenge for many people with a Yellow personality type. When I think of a Yellow leader, I think of Richard Branson, a thrill-seeker who flits from industry to industry. They are enthusiastic, optimistic, and great at drumming up excitement, but they often don't know what to do with all that momentum once they've created it. Follow-through is a real challenge for Yellow types.

While everyone has one fundamental core motivation (and thus one type) that they are born with, many people are also strongly affected by other types. Even if a motivation is not intrinsic to a person, they can have it embedded within them by years of repetition and normalization. If you are a White, for example, drawn to peace and repelled by disharmony, but you grow up in an overwhelmingly Red atmosphere, you may learn to pursue power because everyone around you does so. You may force yourself to be decisive, to engage in conflict because you have no other frame of reference for the world. You may have some distant sense that you are not exactly happy with the things you are pursuing, but if you don't actually understand what you want and why you want it, you can't break free from that Red environment in which you're trapped.

In my particular case, when I was in the corporate world, I was a Blue personality who was consistently getting criticized for some very Red flaws. In performance reviews, I was getting hammered with accusations that I was insensitive, arrogant, and unwilling to compromise. I was driving away people who should have been my teammates with my aggressive, self-focused leadership style. We call this "incongruence" when others see us as a specific personality type with specific motivations that are in conflict with our true motivations.

When I first heard these criticisms, I didn't truly "hear" them. In the business world, the limitations that we see in so many people are instead called "blind spots." I was truly blind to the negative impact my choices were having upon others. Instead, I thought the critiques were misguided or made in bad faith. I refused to believe that I might actually have these problems because, if I believed that, I would have to change and changing required looking inward, something I was absolutely not prepared to do.

I had grown up in a situation where Red goals and Red methods of leadership were paramount. My father's sense of how to be a leader came largely from his own experience in the military (a Red atmosphere, if there ever was one!). I was shown from a very early age that power, domination, and hierarchy were important. The things that I truly valued in my heart of hearts, like deepening relationships and connecting with others, were treated as, at best, something of negligible value and, at worst, a weakness. Ironically, the Blue types can arguably be seen as the most "powerful" because the connections we forge and the emotions that we nurture can motivate and shape people in incredible ways that a more traditional Red leader cannot understand.

Still, I could not help but be influenced by all the messages I was getting from authority figures in my life. Thus, when it came time for me, as an adult, to take on leadership roles, I didn't gravitate toward a management style that suited my instincts; I did what I had been taught to do and I was destroying everything. In my marriage, in my career, I was acting according to a set of values that did not truly make me feel happy or fulfilled and did not make me an effective leader, teammate, or partner to the people around me. I had been a "shining star" for much of my career and I had incredible successes but, somehow, I still found myself bumping up against the same limitations, time after time.

I was hard-driving and self-focused and I pushed people as hard as I possibly could. I was completely poisoning the valuable relationships in my life. My first marriage failed in no small part because I was interpreting everything through the lens of myself and my needs, and constantly urging my wife to grow and change and develop on my timeline instead of hers. I struggled to make the relationships in her life and her family work, even though many of those connections just weren't healthy for any of us.

At work, I was burning people out and frustrating them. I struggled to rise beyond the VP level because I could not get a team to cohere around me. When I finally became a CEO for the first time, I almost lost that role for the same reason, until I discovered how lost I was in my own limitations, and realized what I needed to do to address the problem: a process Dr. Hartman would call "become charactered."

The worst part of all this struggle was that none of this made me feel satisfied. Even when I got the results I wanted, I still felt anxious and hunted. I may have known how to talk the Red talk but when it came time to walk the walk, I still had my inner Blue framework. I couldn't make the confident snap decisions that a good Red leader can make. I couldn't see a clear pathway from where I was to where I wanted to be. Red people are frequently bridge builders; they see an obstacle and figure out a way to get over it. I was standing on the shore, terrified of the river in front of me, unable to formulate a plan.

I was crippled by uncertainty, indecision, and fear of the future. I've often said that a Blue personality who hasn't confronted his or her limitations might long to climb Mount Everest but would never make it past Base Camp, as a result of becoming too obsessed with problems twenty, ten, or even just five steps down the line. Every time I had to make a major decision, I felt like I was poised there at the base of the mountain, terrified of the choices I hadn't even made yet. I was so stuck that I couldn't properly access the incredible blessings of a Blue personality, including quality, service, and empathy.

Part of my problem was that I was not directing my energies in the right place. There was something in me that longed to do a different type of work, something involving teaching or exchanging ideas. What I really wanted was to get out there and connect with people in meaningful ways and see that I was having a positive impact upon their lives. I could do the corporate-executive thing—I had been doing for several years, in fact—but it was not my true purpose and it did not nourish me in the way my later work has done.

A large part of changing my life and my destructive behaviors was honestly determining what I really valued as opposed to the things I believed I was *supposed* to value. I had a moment of recognition when I did Tony Robbins's values exercise and discovered that "love" did not appear in my list of values. Nor did "gratitude" or "closeness." My top value was actually "significance." I truly believed that it was important for me to have the nicest car, the fanciest job title, the biggest salary. Except that, as time went on and I accrued more and more of those very things, I realized that they weren't fulfilling me; they weren't making me feel accomplished and nourished. I had been taught all my life that wielding power over others was how you established yourself as a leader and man and, now that I did have power, all I felt was emptiness.

I was slowly realizing that what I had thought were essential truths of the world were, in reality, myths. I thought that the "quality" of a life was measured in the square footage of a home or the price of a car. In practice, however, I was abandoning my spouse and my children in pursuit of more and more *stuff* that gave me no joy and no sense of fulfillment. I couldn't help but think that there had to be a different path for me.

I had been pushing down my real wants and needs for so long that, if you had asked me directly, I would no longer have been able to identify what I truly wanted from my life. I was fumbling toward someone else's goals, using the most caustic tools I had been given, and if I wanted to lead a truly satisfying life, everything would have to change.

I had to start by acknowledging the limitations both of my natural Blue-leaning personality and of the Red overlay rooted in my upbringing. There was a tendency in me toward arrogance, toward selfishness, and toward a certain disregard for the happiness and comfort of people on my team (whether that team was at work or at home). Those were potential trouble spots that I would have to be cognizant of and try to avoid.

At the same time, I also had a lot of the classic Blue-type flaws. I was prone to worry, obsessive about projects and about relationships, indecisive, and unable to draw solid boundaries. Once I was able to recognize these limitations, I was actually able to make the other personality types work for me by highlighting the strengths of each type and attempting to reduce the weaknesses. I worked to integrate some of the Red-style assertiveness in my life generally, creating clear boundaries and enforcing them when necessary.

I used to have the problem of allowing myself to become overburdened with work. My bosses would delegate too many tasks for me or create situations where I was forced to work after hours and on weekends to complete projects and I wouldn't be able to assert myself and resist these intrusions into my time. I used some of that Red positive self-interest and tenacity to firmly indicate that certain times—nights and weekends—were reserved for my family and I would complete my work during work hours. Often, my bosses and I both found that the work I did in this fashion was far superior to the stuff I resentfully churned out during some sunny

Sunday afternoon on which I would rather have been spending time with my children.

At the same time, I could apply some of that Blue relationship building to these teams that I had to manage. I was able to establish a better rapport with people and I discovered that instead of using intimidation and aggressiveness to push them further and further, I could get incredible work out of people who felt a sense of loyalty and connection to me.

The more of that kind of work I did, the more I realized that I actually wanted to spend my time working with people on a more personally significant level. The corporate world just wasn't giving me the opportunities to do the things that I was best at and even though I had made a lot of positive changes, I could not help but feel that being a CEO, being a business leader, just wasn't a healthy thing for me to do. I was trying to cram a square peg into a round hole when I was living in the corporate world, and changing industries felt like standing up and stretching after an interminable car ride. It was incredible how good it felt to simply be at home in my own skin.

Later, I came to the realization that it wasn't necessarily the office of CEO that was so bad for me—I did both want and need a guiding, leadership position—but that the way I was doing it just wasn't working. I needed to come at the issue of leadership from more of a "charactered" perspective, taking into account the things that mattered most to me, including forging positive relationships, truly helping people, and being a force of positive growth in the lives of others. Unfortunately, that wasn't the way I was trying to lead people earlier in my career.

If I had never learned how to find out what motivates me, and if I had never developed the fortitude necessary to do that work, I would probably still be on the corporate treadmill today. I would be sick; distanced from the people whom I loved; always struggling to get more, do more, have more; and still feeling hollowed out. The worst part is, I would never be able to understand why I didn't feel good when I had all the things I thought I was supposed to have.

The first story in this book is about a boy who has been dealt a difficult hand in life. His story is specific but it is also generally applicable. There are millions of people out in the world right now dealing with similar wounds; there are people struggling with abuse, with addiction, with mental illness, with trauma of all varieties. There are people who are even just struggling with a deep sense of ignorance about their truest self, a fundamental confusion about who they are and why they make the choices they make. In order to find purpose, we need to discover the hurt inside, get angry about it, and then face those emotions head on. Most of us keep the past buried in a misguided attempt to avoid showing vulnerability and, as a result, most people never truly live with real passion and real purpose.

Imagine that boy growing up, launching relationships, and heading into the workforce. Imagine him never knowing that things could be different, that he could live a life unconcerned with gaining and keeping power. Imagine no one ever giving him the tools he needs to identify the motive that drives him. What a sad story that would be.

My story is not a sad story; it's an incredibly joyful one. It is a triumphant story, what Joseph Campbell would have called a "Hero's Journey," and there is no reason at all that your story can't also be a Hero's Journey. If you are reading this book, that means you've already taken a big step: you are willing to look inward, even though the idea is frightening. Joseph Campbell identified a number of specific moments in a narrative that define a Hero's Journey and one of the first and most significant is what he termed "The Call to Adventure." This is when something major happens in the ordinary world that a character occupies; it might be positive (though it is usually negative) but, either way, it is dramatic and it demands action. How the individual chooses to respond to this demand is what sets him on his journey to acquire new wisdom and knowledge; it is what makes him a Hero.

So, here is the challenge, the demand, the adventure. How will you respond?

THE AXEMAN

I want him gone."

The company's president looked smaller behind his desk. Undoubtedly, that was not his intention but the big expanse of gleaming glass and polished wood only highlighted his short stature, his relatively squat build. For all that, he was still intimidating—like a bulldog or one of those bullet-headed terriers, something compact and strong and vicious when it wanted to be.

"What exactly is the issue?" Alex shifted uncomfortably in his seat.

The president fixed his attention on him like a laser, like he was trying to bore through him. It was a move common to many corporate leaders but one that Alex had never really gotten used to.

"The issue is, he's not doing his damn job. I put him on a project; he says he's gonna do it but when the deadline rolls around, he's got nothing. He lies right to my face and I can't stand it. Reminds me of my oldest son."

"Your manager has a good reputation," Alex pointed out. He'd done some research on the man before coming to this meeting and it seemed that he had worked on a number of successful projects with other companies. There were no major red flags in his work history.

"Apparently not with me," the president said darkly. "I need someone I can trust in this position. Talking to him . . ." His face screwed up with consternation. "It's like throwing stones into a bottomless pit. You just keep putting stuff in and . . . nothing."

"Well, let me talk with him, get the lay of the land and we'll see about resolving this." Alex was careful not to make any promises in either direction. It was his job, ideally, to heal ruptures in team cohesion, not to fire people indiscriminately.

The president shrugged and smiled. Despite his bulldog appearance, he still had a wolfish smile.

"Well, you're the expert, right? *The Axeman?*"

The Axeman. Because he came in and cut away all the dead weight, leaving only the healthy parts of the organization behind. It wasn't the nickname he might have picked for himself but people seemed to like it. Maybe he should put it on his business cards?

"Yeah," Alex smiled, "the Axeman."

"You're going to have to pronounce that last name for me, I'm afraid." Alex smiled, sitting down across from the tall, somewhat blank-faced man.

"Afanasyev, but just call me Viktor," he responded immediately with the air of someone who had explained the concept many times before.

"What is that? Ukrainian?"

"Russian," his voice was soft.

Alex was beginning to see what the president had meant about a bottomless pit, Viktor had a remarkably unreadable face. Alex wondered if it was something he came by naturally or something that he had practiced.

"OK, Viktor, how long have you been working here?" It was a question Alex already knew the answer to but these initial assessments were as much about *how* the individual said things as they were about what was actually said.

"Eight months."

Alex let the silence stretch on, but Viktor did not offer any further information. Most people don't like silence; they would rush to fill it if Alex didn't. Viktor just looked at him with that same bland, neutral expression.

"And how have you been liking it?" Alex prompted finally.

"It's a very competitive workplace." Viktor sounded rehearsed. Alex's clients usually had at least some inkling that he was coming in to assess them; apparently, Viktor had taken time to prepare a script for himself. It would be Alex's job to force the man to veer away from that script and speak candidly.

"And the president? How is your relationship with him?"

"He's a very admirable person. He has achieved so much," Viktor said, not answering the question. Yup, this one was going to be a challenge.

Unlike Alex, who worked around the clock for months at a time on an assignment and then had a few weeks of downtime, Sondra had a nine-to-five, the kind of job a kid imagines when he or she thinks of growing up. She worked in a bank, she was three years younger than Alex and they had been living together for six months. He liked to watch her get ready for work in the mornings, flitting back and forth from the bathroom to the bedroom. Every time she emerged from the bathroom, she would have applied some new piece of her amour. First her makeup, then her hairstyle, then her sensible, autumn-toned wardrobe, and, finally, her shoes.

"Why do you bother with all that?" he asked, watching as Sondra patiently rolled up a soft pair of fabric flats and tucked them into her purse.

"Stand up all day in these?" she gave him a glittering little laugh and extended one leg to show off her sleek black shoe, balanced on a tall spike of a heel. "No way, José."

She was always so cheerful when she went to work at the bank, one of the few people he knew who seemed to genuinely thrive on all the stressors that came with her job. She was never happier than when she was achieving.

"So why wear them at all, then?"

She just shrugged.

"It's all part of it." Part of the work, she meant, part of the image, part of the job, like the carefully calibrated and only slightly stilted smile she used for all the clients. Or like the way she brought home her work in piles on the weekend even though it was only "suggested" that she do so.

"Oh, it's Thursday, so I expect some of us will be going out. A wine bar opened on the Drive a couple of weeks ago."

Something in him grew tight and painful, like a guitar string stretched nearly to the breaking point.

He tried to sound as casual as possible when he said, "Oh, OK. You have fun."

She looked at him in a way that made him think he wasn't as good at hiding his inner tension as he'd thought and bent down to kiss his cheek.

"You can come, you know. You have a standing invitation."

Alex shook his head.

"Not this time." Not any time. Walking into a bar was, for him, much like walking into a hospital was for other people. He felt . . . unsettled, like there was something prickly underneath his skin. He always found himself looking around, watching everyone closely just in case . . . He didn't know what he was expecting (fearing?), but it was an awful feeling all the same.

He particularly hated watching Sondra drink. She wasn't much of a drinker, as she had reminded him on several occasions, but there was just something about seeing her sip from a glass of wine or, at the worst, a vodka tonic, that made him feel almost physically ill. It was an awful twisting knot in his stomach, nauseating and fearful.

But he could not ask her to miss out on what might be useful networking time with coworkers. He could not ask her to live the way he did, tensing up whenever he smelled the dull, yeasty ferment of beer or the sharp burn of clear liquor.

"Have fun," he said, giving her the best smile he could manage.

He hoped it was enough.

Viktor was talking on the phone. Presumably, it was a private call and he certainly looked as though he was trying to hide it, half hunched with his arms tucked in on himself, like he was trying his mightiest to condense himself into something small, something invisible.

As Alex drew closer to him, he realized that he wasn't speaking English, but a deep, crashing language that Alex presumed was Russian.

Viktor noticed him and his eyes widened. He said something soft into the phone and then pulled it away from his ear, looking down nervously.

"Sorry," he said, "sort of a family emergency."

"I won't bust you," Alex smiled. "I didn't realize you spoke Russian."

"Well, my mother would tell you I don't. Not really. Not properly."

"Sounded good to me!"

Viktor's smile could not have been more forced and awkward if he had pushed up the edges of his mouth with his fingers.

"So your parents are from Russia?" Alex could sense that this was an undesirable topic of conversation for Viktor but that seemed to make it all the more significant.

"Yes. Around Yekaterinburg."

"But you were born here, in Canada?"

Viktor's eyes flicked over his shoulder like he wanted to turn and retreat.

"Yeah," he said uneasily. It was the most blatant display of emotion that Alex had yet seen from him.

"It's tough," Alex offered, "growing up with immigrant parents."

For the first time since the conversation had started, Viktor looked him in the eye. He seemed to be appraising him somehow, taking in Alex's medium-toned skin and dark hair.

"You are . . . ?"

"Little bit of everything," Alex told him cheerfully. "But my mom and dad are Pacific Islanders. We moved here when I was young; we kids all grew up speaking just English, though."

"Me too. My parents didn't want me to have an accent or have trouble in school. Then I grew up and my terrible Russian is just one more way in which I failed them as a son." He smiled when he said it but Alex knew that kind of smile, a thin coating of self-deprecation that covered something deep and bitter. If you weren't looking closely, you could mistake it for a joke.

But Alex was always looking closely. It was his job.

Are you sure you don't wanna come? We can meet up at the bar. I'll give you the address.

He let Sondra's text just sit there, a little green bubble floating in a void. There was a part of him that wanted to answer in the affirmative, that wanted to find the bar and find her. He knew, though, that it wouldn't be to enjoy a night out with his girlfriend. If he went looking for Sondra now, it would be to watch her, to keep tabs on her and make sure she wasn't—wasn't what? Cheating on him?

He had no reason to think that. Sondra had always been honest with him and she'd never showed any interest in other men, not even when they'd showed interest in her. Yet, he could not seem to shake the jealous unease that came upon him almost every time she went out like this. He dwelled obsessively on what she might be doing, out there without him, the stem of a wineglass clutched in her hand. Would she flirt with her coworkers or accept their flirting in kind? Would she let them touch her? Would she forget about the promises she made to him, both explicit and implicit?

He wanted to be asleep when she got home, but he couldn't manage it. After forty-five minutes of tossing restlessly in bed and watching the minutes tick by on the alarm clock, he got up and opened his computer. He reread his files on Viktor, searching for something he had missed.

Viktor had a degree from University of British Columbia. He had launched new products, rolled out company-wide initiatives, and turned around whole departments that had been spiraling before his arrival. He had also gotten married two years ago and, according to his HR record, the two of them were expecting a child.

Perhaps that was what had made Alex so reluctant to do as the company president had asked and just cut their losses, cut Viktor loose. It felt so . . . uncaring to fire a person right before the birth of his first child.

Or maybe it was none of that. Maybe the child was something else, some kind of clue or key. All sorts of things changed when a baby came into the picture. It was like disrupting the silt at the bottom of a pond: all sorts of hidden things came to the surface.

He heard Sondra's key in the door not long after midnight and he didn't know what to do. He thought about shutting his laptop and rolling over in the darkness, taking his breathing slow and pretending to be asleep. It was something he used to do when his dad returned after a night of drinking.

Sometimes his dad had chosen not to wake him up. Sometimes, he had just stood in Alex's doorway, looking at him while swaying ever so slightly. It was almost a loving gesture, a parent watching over his sleeping child. However, Alex had known that, really, his father was just evaluating him, weighing his options. Would it be satisfying to pull his son out of bed? To beat and berate him for some imagined transgression until he'd vented all his bleary rage? Would it make him feel just a little bit better? While he had stood there wondering, Alex had lain there trying to make his breathing as deep and regular as he could manage. He had tried to pretend that he wasn't afraid.

Alex shut his laptop and got out of bed, padding softly into the kitchen where Sondra was getting herself a glass of water. She wasn't wearing any shoes now, her heels dangling from one loose hand. Her hair had deflated slightly from the exertions of the day and she had a little bit of redness in her cheeks, a little glassiness to her eyes. That was the only real indication she'd had anything to drink.

"Hi, sweetie," she said, looking surprised albeit pleased to see him. "I didn't wake you, did I?" Her voice was steady and clear, she wasn't slurring, and her motions as she shut off the tap and took a long drink were sure and controlled.

"No," Alex said, unable to keep the tightness out of his voice. "How much did you have to drink tonight?" He winced as he asked the question. It seemed to erupt out of him, beyond his control.

"Uh . . . a couple of glasses of wine. Why do you ask?" Sondra's eyes widened and she appeared bewildered.

Alex felt like he was ambushing her. Maybe he was.

"What's a couple? Two?"

"That is the generally accepted meaning of the word 'couple,' yes," Sondra snapped, no longer looking bewildered. "Why are you asking me this?" She was angry and there was some part of Alex that thought her anger might be justified, but another part, a much stronger part, bristled at her.

"Because I can tell. I can tell from your face and your voice that you've been drinking."

Sondra's eyes narrowed.

"Yes, I had a drink. I just told you that."

"*One* drink? I thought you said two?"

"It was rhetorical!" Sondra threw up her hands and nearly spilled her glass of water. Alex reached out to take it from her. She scowled and held it up, out of his reach. "I'm not a child, I don't need you to hold on to my sippy cup."

"No, you're not a child; you're a—"

Alex didn't finish his sentence but that didn't mean that the both of them didn't hear exactly what he meant. Sondra gave him a long, searching look.

"What did I do?" she asked, her voice small and aching. "Why are you mad at me?"

He wasn't mad at her, not at Sondra who got up two hours before him on the weekends to make pancakes with strawberries in them, who had convinced him to start running half marathons again, who read aloud to him at night from whatever book she'd been absorbed in that week. He wasn't mad at the *real* Sondra but he knew from experience that alcohol could transform a person.

That was what his father had always said: "It wasn't me. That was someone else." That was how he'd apologized to Alex's mother, by blaming the other man, the one who lived in the bottle.

"I have to get up early tomorrow," he said, turning away from her before she had a chance to respond.

———————

"A . . . a girl," Viktor told him. He seemed surprised that Alex would ask.

"Congratulations. Got any names picked out yet?"

The corners of Viktor's mouth turned down very slightly in his version of a frown.

"None that we can agree on. My wife thinks we should name her after my mother but . . . "

"But you don't like that?"

Viktor shook his head.

"My older brother named his first kid after our father. I never understood that. That man made our life hell, I couldn't see why he'd want to honour him like that."

Alex watched Viktor carefully as he spoke, looking for even a hint of an expression. He thought he saw something like recognition in the other man's eyes.

"My mother is . . . a very angry person." Viktor lowered his voice although the two of them were alone. Maybe this was something he could only speak of in whispers. "It didn't matter what I did—or didn't do—I always made her so *mad.*"

Mad enough to hit you? Alex wondered.

"When my dad got angry," Alex chose each word carefully, "nothing made him feel better than knocking his kids around."

It was as though something had passed between them, either above or below the level of words, and Viktor now had permission to speak, permission to feel, permission to let some of those feelings show on his face.

"My mother always hit me with *things.* Belts, sticks, shoes, cords, whatever was close when she got in a mood. Later, she'd take care of me bare-handed, putting on band-aids, Neosporin, holding a half-frozen washcloth to my bruises." While he was talking, he reached up and touched his left cheekbone. It looked like an involuntary action, like he didn't even realize what he was doing. Alex wondered fleetingly what things his own body did automatically when he remembered his father.

"But that wasn't the worst thing. The worst thing was the sound. She was always yelling, always so damn loud, always angry. All I ever really wanted was silence. Peace."

———————

"I don't think you ought to let him go."

The company president had seemed so cheerful when Alex had entered his office. His smile slipped away now, and was replaced by a deep frown that wore creases in the side of his face.

"So you got through to him?" The president didn't sound particularly happy about the idea.

"I think *you* can get through to him. If you follow my advice."

The president leaned back against his desk and spread his hands in an "I'm waiting," gesture.

"You're hard-charging and aggressive," Alex began. "It's served you well in your career and it's a big part of why you are where you are." He gestured around the room, at the gleaming furniture, at the window taller than two men standing one on top of the other. "When someone comes at you, really gets in your face, it fires you up and makes you want to achieve. But Viktor isn't like you. He thinks differently; he values different things."

The president looked skeptical but he was still listening. Alex thought that was a good sign.

"When you challenge Viktor, all he sees is that aggression and it paralyzes him. He doesn't feel galvanized; he feels fear and it's that fear that is keeping him from delivering."

Alex was afraid that the president was going to dismiss him entirely from the hard way that he was staring at him. But when the president spoke, there was something hopeful, even sunny, in his voice.

"OK," he said, "what do I do?"

Alex smiled.

"You have to learn to speak his language."

———————

"What's this?" It was the first thing Sondra had said to him since their blowout earlier in the week. Well, the first thing other than "excuse me" or "I already took out the garbage" or any of the other purely functional phrases she offered in a curt monotone.

She had been unpacking the last of their moving boxes, one of his, apparently, judging by the small model car in her hand.

"That's a 1958 Corvette Roadster."

"Did you make it?" she held the little car up and peered at the underside.

"I put it together. It came in a kit. I used to have a lot of them."

"This is the only one I've seen."

Alex shrugged, trying to be easy and casual.

"That one was my favorite. Got rid of most of the rest of them."

She moved toward him and he could still see the hesitancy in her body language.

"Do you want to put it up somewhere? Like a display?"

She half held the car out to him but Alex couldn't quite bring himself to take it.

"My dad used to buy those for me," he said. Sondra just looked at him, creating a silence that he rushed to fill. "He knew I liked them, so he would get them as a kind of . . . apology after he'd done something. Gotten drunk and broken something of mine, gotten drunk and hit me, gotten drunk and cheated on mom. When I was really little, I thought it meant just what he said it did, that it was an apology and his way of, you know, loving me. When I got older, I started to wonder if he wasn't giving me things to love just so he'd have more things to destroy."

Sondra looked down at the model car like it was carved from a delicate sheet of the finest crystal.

"You never told me that," she said softly.

Alex thought of Viktor and his daughter who still didn't have a name. He thought of the company president who pushed and shouted but, ultimately, wanted his employees to succeed. He thought about how a person could see shadows—ghosts—of his own problems just about anywhere, if that's what he wanted to see.

"Yeah," Alex said, "I should have told you a long time ago."

2 PHASE TWO
THE
VISION

What is the purpose of this life?
What is your passion?

I've heard the call to adventure in my own life, not just once or twice, but countless times. Often, I've ignored the prompts and just kept doggedly moving forward with whatever I was doing at the time, certain that if I just did the same thing enough times with enough dedication, I would break through the walls that seemed to pop up everywhere. Other times, I heard the call and I convinced myself that I was answering it. The problem was, I lacked the introspection necessary to understand what would really bring me satisfaction in my life, so I would do things that I *thought* were important and meaningful, but which really just left me feeling hollow.

I had not discovered my purpose.

That's not at all uncommon. Napoleon Hill of *Think and Grow Rich* fame claims that a full 95 percent of people never discover their real purpose in life. These people move through life in a way that might seem normal and functional from the outside but, in their hearts and in their minds, they are racked with a kind of stifled desperation. People who never confront this desperation instead become angry, sometimes even convincing themselves that they never really wanted anything other than what they currently have.

Everyone wants the feeling of clarity and rightness that comes from finding one's purpose and working toward it. Every person wants his or her life and choices to feel meaningful. When we don't have that important feeling, we suffer. We suffer in our work and we suffer in our personal lives. Even our bodies suffer.

Some people are lucky enough to know from a very early age exactly what they need—not just want, but *need*—to do in this world. I was privileged to meet one such individual, Baraladei Daniel Igali a freestyle wrestler who brought home Canada's very first gold medal in the sport of wrestling. Daniel is a sports icon in Canada and so when I had the chance to sit down with him, I jumped at the opportunity.

I am always curious about the driving forces that push high-level athletes who often spend years training relentlessly for one specific competition or moment in time, so I asked Daniel why he had been so dedicated to that gold medal and what had pushed him onward.

He explained to me that when he was growing up in Nigeria, he didn't really have an understanding or awareness of the Olympics. The entire country struggled with crippling poverty, food was scarce, and safety was by no means assured. One often hears stories about elite athletes who spend day and night on the balance beam, or in the pool from the time they are small children, but Daniel didn't really have that luxury. His earliest exposure to wrestling came from impromptu play with other children, but he knew, even then, that wrestling made him feel more satisfied—more complete—than anything else in his life.

The call to adventure came in early for Daniel and he followed it unhesitatingly. Despite struggling with food insecurity, poverty, and the looming threat of political instability, he was determined to climb to the very highest levels of his chosen profession, even if he'd have to travel halfway across the world to do it!

Now, Daniel's knowledge of what he needed to do didn't make it *easy* to do and there were plenty of obstacles along the way. There were plenty of people who either tried to dissuade him from his goals or to convince him that what he was doing was crazy and that he would never get the outcome he wanted. Daniel had to be strong enough to power through the challenges that came with being from a "Third World" country as well as all the conventional wisdom that said a kid in Nigeria with limited access to resources could never wind up on an Olympic podium.

Daniel could not change many of the circumstances of his life. He could not change the economic situation of his country. He could not purchase better facilities or coaches. He could not make the Olympic bureaucracy easier to navigate or mitigate his need to balance his training with providing for himself and his family and ensuring their safety. He could control himself, however. He could choose how he reacted to these challenges and whether he would quit or forge ahead. To do that, he leaned heavily upon his feeling of purpose, which was always with him like a hot coal in his belly, a burning desire within that urged him onward. It was still a long and difficult path he had set himself upon but simply knowing that it was the *right* path made it worthwhile.

These days, Daniel has dedicated himself to helping children in his home country. He wants to remove some of the barriers that he had to muscle his way through so that the next time a young man or woman in Nigeria dreams of competing at the highest levels, it won't be considered just a pipe dream. It will be exactly what it should be: a worthwhile goal that is achievable with talent, hard work, and purpose.

Daniel is an exceptional person in many ways, not the least of which is that driving purpose and how early in his life he discovered it. Not all of us have that kind of clarity and determination, especially at such a young age; however, many people I know who have also found their purpose tell similar stories of already knowing what they wanted—and doing it—in their earliest childhood. Sometimes the daily demands of our lives can actually obscure our original passions, responsibilities, and expectations—calcifying around us until we are nearly unrecognizable. I have discovered, though, that just as life draws us away from the things that mean the most to us, it can also offer us multiple chances to discover our true purpose.

I thought I knew my purpose when I was a teenager and my father finally left us: I had to get a good job and help take care of everyone. I had to prove to my dad that I could be the only kind of man he'd ever respected: the powerful kind with lots of money and lots of material possessions.

I went into the work force right out of high school (there was no money for college, though many of my teachers suggested that I go to business school) and I wound up working as a bank teller—and then manager—for a company called National Trust. I rose quickly through the ranks there and I found that the work was coming very easily to me. It was true what my teacher had said: I had an eye for business. I was only a few years out of high school but I was already making good money and on the fast track to bigger and better positions.

I was a manager by the time I hit my early twenties and then, in quick succession, a director, a vice president, and, finally, a CEO when I was still only in my thirties. I moved through five different business sectors and served in almost every corporate capacity during my journey. I was experiencing incredible monetary and professional success.

After one of my first significant bonuses, I purchased an apartment for my mother and helped her fix it up. It was intended to be a place of her own, a place where she could feel safe from the worries of unpaid bills or legal fees. In the end, it didn't quite turn out that way, but just being able to procure that living space for her felt like an important step in my life.

It should have felt good. I was making money, which was something that my father had always considered the primary marker of success, and I was providing for my mother in the way I thought I was meant to do. Yet, on those rare occasions when I allowed myself to look inward, I felt a darkness and a nothingness there. I didn't like myself. My achievements didn't make me feel good. I was following the advice I had been given by the people in my life, however flawed and limited it may have been, but I was not happy.

Since that time, I have heard hundreds of variations on that story. Most people don't really examine why it is that they entered their chosen careers. Too often, it's simply because that whatever he or she is doing was the easiest thing to do. Maybe he runs a restaurant or a small business because that's what his parents did. Maybe she's a doctor or a lawyer because everyone always told her those were "safe" professions. Maybe he's a teacher or an accountant or a middle manager because someone along the way said he was good at it. In all these cases, when it came time to make a choice about the future, each person took the path of least resistance, and he or she kept taking it, day after day, year after year, only to wake up one day and discover that the path had veered off wildly. That person no longer had any idea where he or she was, or, more tragically, where he or she even *wanted* to be.

That is a scary idea, and coming to terms with it means coming to terms with the idea that something major has to change in your life—another scary idea. So when I was confronted with this early in my career, I did what a lot of people do: I pushed it down and ignored it. In fact, I doubled down on my career, using a merger between National Trust and a larger banking conglomerate to climb even further up the corporate ladder. It meant that money was my whole world. I spent my days managing a lending portfolio, trying to grow other people's money so I could make a larger salary for myself. It meant staying quiet and pretending to laugh when my boss cheerfully called me "our token nigger" in a room full of executives. It meant deferring to men who went out of their way to disrespect me and make it clear that, as a brown person, I was always going to be a guest in their house, dependent upon their largesse.

I thought, though, if I could just rise high enough, become wealthy enough, then these indignities wouldn't matter. On that day, when I had finally achieved enough, I would be able to look at myself and my life and not feel disappointment.

These feelings should have been red flags. It wasn't *just* that I encountered prejudice in the workplace or had difficulty working with others in the office in the first third of my career. If my true purpose was to be a CEO and head up a corporation, those would be legitimate challenges that I needed to overcome to meet my goal, the same way that Daniel had to contend with limited resources and safety issues. The problem was how those things made me feel. I wasn't like Daniel, I didn't have a burning, constant sense of purpose to comfort me through these things. I was struggling to work with others because I was trying desperately to be the kind of person I thought I was supposed to be—a high-achieving, ultra-aggressive Red CEO type—rather than allowing myself to be the person I was. A quality- and service-oriented Blue personality who felt dehumanized by the racial slurs and the accusations that I was a "token" rather than a valuable team member who earned his position through hard work and constant relationship building. In those days, I would have said I did that to help my team meet our goals but I can see now that I was fueled, even then, by a desire for intimacy and I was using that strength instinctively.

I wasn't at a place in my life where I could critique the goals I'd set for myself but as the years went on and my unhappiness swelled, I had to acknowledge that something was wrong. So, I did what I had been taught to do in my youth: I found fault with myself. If leadership positions and big salaries weren't making me happy, it couldn't possibly be that those things were not of fundamental importance to me. Those things were important to everyone! No, it had to be something wrong with my personality, with my way of understanding things.

Counterintuitively, I began to use work to hide from my unhappiness, a large part of which was caused by the work I was doing. By the time I was in my thirties, I had married my second wife, Anna. She was a few years older than me and she brought her two young sons to the relationship, as well as their shared history with her husband, a domineering and abusive Italian man. Anna's parents were also Italian and she had been raised in a family where a certain degree of assertiveness in men when communicating verbally is considered normal and healthy. Because of this, it took some time for her to recognize that what her husband was doing went beyond the bounds of acceptable behavior for a spouse. By then, though, the damage had been done to all of them.

When we first got married, I thought for sure that it was meant to be. I looked at her sons, wary and full of an anger that they could barely understand, let alone articulate, and I saw my brothers and myself. I thought that marrying her and parenting those boys would be like getting the chance to do what no one did for me: step in and help everyone heal.

My career wasn't completely fulfilling, that was true, but I told myself that if I could fix these people and pull us together into a family, that would make me feel whole and happy. *That* would be my purpose.

I forgot that it's really, really hard to fix someone else's trauma when you haven't really dealt with your own. I had been out of my father's house for years and I was a successful adult in my own right, but the weight of my childhood was still with me. Struggling to help Anna's sons invariably brought all of those feelings and memories to the surface and I was completely compromised. I would go into challenging interactions with the boys as a raw nerve, feeling ten years old, myself. It was exactly the wrong way to approach parenting and, instead of addressing the problem, I started working long into the night or going in early in the morning. I could not have admitted it to myself, but I was avoiding my family. I felt like I was failing them, failing in what I had decided was my primary purpose: to fix them and erase their past.

Of course, no one could actually do that and that wasn't what Anna and the kids needed from me, but I couldn't accept that. I couldn't even really name the emotions I was experiencing. I had become so alienated from myself and my feelings after years and years of trying desperately to pretend that I wasn't really sad or ashamed or frustrated or disappointed.

We might have continued that way, struggling with problems that we didn't fully understand and, in my case, couldn't even put a real name to, but instead, there came one more Call to Adventure. And this one was the biggest, most unignorable one yet.

In the mid to late 2000s, several huge changes happened to our family in short succession. First, I lost my job as an executive at TELUS, a telecommunications company that was struggling to shore up a falling stock price (which was a direct result of major strategic changes that the company was making, undermining shareholder confidence). It wasn't entirely unexpected, part of working as an executive is making your peace with the fact that your career is entirely subject to the fortunes of the company in general. Plus, at that time, I was primarily working as a "change agent" or someone who comes into an existing company and helps it successfully make changes that will, ideally, make it a better, more profitable entity. This was particularly critical in telecommunications, an industry that was changing quickly at that time. People with my job description tended to have shorter three- or four-year positions, rather than sitting in the same job for decades. In fact, the faster a change agent could transform a company, the better their reputation. My reputation was very good. I even acquired a nickname: "Tommy Gun," because I was a hired gun often called in to fix situations that could not be addressed by the in-house team.

The downside of this type of work was that my positions were brief and I occasionally had to hustle to pick up another job after one was completed. After TELUS let me go, I did my best to turn the situation around. I began reaching out to my contacts in various industries and letting them know I was on the market. I eventually landed a CEO position at what had, until recently, been a collection of independently run companies across Canada. A large American company had absorbed it and removed the existing president, causing chaos. Customers were defecting and the temporary company head they had put in place wasn't local and was attempting to do damage control from afar. I was brought in as vice president with the understanding that, if I could stabilize the company and make it profitable, I would be promoted to CEO.

To say that the company was already in crisis mode when I arrived would be an understatement. The former owners of the company had actually locked the doors of the building in an attempt to resolve the abrupt change in leadership, and an ensuing lawsuit soon arose between the Canadian and American companies. The termination of the CEO was enormously unpopular and a good 80 percent of the company's existing client base was threatening to leave over the former CEO being ousted. They were personal friends of the old CEO and were willing to walk, out of loyalty to him.

My first task was wooing those clients back. The company sold insurance and had a number of separate agencies run autonomously. The new American owners wanted to reorganize the company into a direct sales force that could eventually be rolled into one national company. It was that single national company that I was really tasked with building, but first, I would have to make this particular company profitable enough to justify the cost.

I used this long-term plan when I met with the existing clients who were looking to pull the plug. I created a PowerPoint and went on a road tour, sharing my vision of this new, stronger company (one which would only come into existence if I could turn the current floundering situation around). I was in a constant state of stress, asking these clients to give our company a second chance and trying to sell them on a future that was not at all certain. I had only my own drive and conviction to sustain me. In the end, I managed to retain about 80 percent of the original customer base.

While all of this was happening, the American company had also given me an alternate assignment: I needed to nail down one major new client worth about $10 million. If I could do that, they would allocate $5 million to me to restructure and rebuild the company into the success that I had promised for so many others.

It was not the kind of position I would have necessarily chosen for myself; it promised to be a lot of work for a very uncertain outcome, but after losing my previous job, I no longer had the luxury of picking and choosing. So I got to work. I developed a new business plan and aggressively courted the new client, and I did indeed bring in that $10 million worth of new business. Then the real work began.

With my rebuilding fund, I began hiring vice presidents and really transforming the company from the DNA level. Throughout that first year, I was essentially carrying the company on my back, making all the major decisions, overseeing everything, and taking a seat at every table. The strain of it was literally killing me. I was only in my thirties, but I was overweight with spiking cholesterol levels, and I was exhausted all the time. A medication I was taking for my high cholesterol actually caused what I later discovered was a near stroke.

I spent what felt like 60 percent of my life on planes, flying from one meeting to another, and even when I was in my home city, I spent most of my time in the office. By this time, Anna and I had a young daughter of our own, Kalinda. We were delighted by her arrival, especially after an earlier pregnancy had ended in a medically necessary termination of what was to be my son, little "Tommy." With my new job, however, I barely got to see my daughter. I joked that I was a frequent flyer, not a frequent father, but the reality wasn't funny at all. For the first five years of my daughter's life, I was more like an uncle or a cousin than a father, popping in periodically for a few days before heading out again.

I told myself that it was OK because this was an important job, the kind of job I was supposed to have. The kind of which my father would have approved. Plus, I was making a quarter of a million dollars a year; surely that was worth more to my daughter than some incidental father-daughter time.

This was another time in my life when I ran straight into the conflict between what I should be feeling and my actual emotions. I should have been on top of the world. I had nearly single-handedly turned around a whole company and made it profitable again, my bosses loved me, and I was making money hand over fist. All I felt, however, was sick and empty and lonely.

At this same time, my wife, Anna, got some devastating news about her mother. She'd had a massive stroke and it had left her with profoundly damaged motor function and unable to speak. My wife was distraught, though she tried to maintain an outward appearance of calm and strength.

I knew she was worried not only for her mother, but for her father as well. In Italian families, the mother is the locus of the family and Anna's family was no exception. Her parents had been married for more than fifty years and her mother had always taken care of everything on the home front. This was a traditional marriage of love and shared roles; however, her mom held more of the domestic duties in the home. Now, she couldn't even take care of herself and Anna's eighty-year-old father was left alone in a house where he couldn't so much as operate the washing machine and missed her mom's love and support.

When I moved off into other industries, Anna remained in the banking industry. She was still with the same bank where we had met and, by this time, she had logged thirty years with them. Like me, she had started working as a teller right out of high school and was quickly promoted to management. She was very successful and sought-after as a manager, and there were many people who considered her a trusted advisor and integral part of the decision-making processes for the bank. There were opportunities for her to move into an executive position but her strong sense of family and work-life balance would preclude her from having the time and flexibility required to provide a good home for her boys. Nevertheless, she had proven herself to be a faithful, talented, and intelligent employee and a long-time asset to the bank. We both believed that she had earned some consideration from her employer during a one-time family emergency but we soon found out that the bank did not feel the same way.

Anna started getting flack for leaving work early or coming in late. There was no accommodation for the fact that she was now serving as a caregiver for her elderly mother and father, and it killed me to see her being treated that way. Anna is strong but she's not made of stone, the constant insinuations that she was not fulfilling her schedule at the bank were just too much for her to bear on top of her father's situation. Anna is a Red personality with a strong Yellow component; I was actually very surprised to discover that she was not an executive when I met her. Reds typically charge ahead without letting internal and external issues hold them back from achieving in the workplace. I think the strong family-first values that Anna was raised with occasionally forced her to make a choice between her family and her career. Unfortunately, people who prioritize caring for their family (especially women) are often penalized in the workplace and, for Anna, that was definitely true.

Anna and I both agreed that something had to give, as she was being pulled in too many directions. We had a robust savings account and extensive lines of credit. I was making that quarter-million a year and we had two houses, one of them worth more than a million dollars. We both agreed that she take an early retirement package from the bank and devote her time to being with her parents. As it turned out, her mother only lived another two years and Anna was very glad that she was able to take that time to be with her.

The bank gave Anna about $200,000, a sum that is called a pension rollover. Most people put that money into some sort of investment package and use the proceeds to live off of in retirement. Considering our other assets and my rock-solid CEO position, though, we weren't too worried.

Around this time, the global economy was changing fast and not always for the better. As an insurance company, we were feeling all the fiscal ups and downs, both at home and abroad. My immediate bosses at the American parent company were feeling a lot of heat from the people who were overseeing them and it felt like every day there was more pressure to cut costs and boost our bottom line. The company was actually finally profitable, but it felt like that profit was never enough and I was always very aware of how critical the situation in the larger company was.

So I did whatever it took. I fired forty people, people I knew personally and with whom I had developed working relationships. I eliminated an entire call center shortly before Christmas and, afterward, I fixated on one young woman who was visibly pregnant. I thought about her and her unborn child and I couldn't sleep.

Shortly thereafter, the order came down that our company was going to be part of a three-way transition with a tech company. It was a huge change and it would require a full restructuring as well as the dismissal of one of my VPs. I was at least able to prepare a package for her, and I was ready to do that; I had the envelope in my hand when I went in to a meeting with my boss. When I walked into the room and saw the representative from HR, a friend of mine whom I had actually hired, I knew what was going to happen. Instead of giving someone a meaningful envelope, I received one myself. Instead of firing an employee, I was fired. As it turned out, the restructuring was even more extensive than I'd realized. Not only was I removed, my entire executive team was eliminated and the corporate office was moved back East. I wasn't just fired; my entire Western Canada-based job no longer existed.

I knew that the corporate world was not looking out for the individual. I knew it when I was a young man and executives dismissed and denigrated me because of my background, and I knew it when TELUS unceremoniously fired me and thousands of others in a vain attempt to halt a falling stock price caused by too much change too quickly. Knowing that, however, didn't make it hurt any less. After building this company basically from the dirt up, my career was ended as part of an attempt to squeeze just a few more dollars out of an already profitable enterprise. The worst part was the realization that I had fired all of those people. I had squeezed and pushed and cut and done things that had kept me up at night, and kept me away from my wife and little girl, and it didn't matter at all. None of it saved me.

Losing that job stung but I had lost jobs before and I might have bounced back in the same way I had in the past, if not for one more major setback.

Back when we were looking into managing Anna's pension fund and figuring out how to invest our combined money, we found an investment program called the Institute for Financial Learning. We'd heard about it through some neighbors of ours whom we trusted and, after doing some research, we decided that the IFFL was the best place to grow our money. So we went all in. We put all of Anna's pension in IFFL and all of our joint savings, every penny we had.

Six months later, we woke up to discover that we were two of more than four thousand investors who had been swindled by IFFL in what was called the largest Ponzi scheme in North American history. In the end, they stole more than $2 billion globally. Just in North America, more than four thousand investors were defrauded to the tune of about $400 million, and everything Anna and I had had was included somewhere in there.

Shortly thereafter, I lost my CEO position. We went from $350 thousand per year to zero. Anna was retired, I was fired, and we lost every penny we had saved over the years. The boys were still in high school, our daughter was still in grade school, and we had no idea what we were going to do.

Shell-shocked, we began the painful process of selling off everything we still owned. Away went the million-dollar house, the second home by the lake, and the fancy cars. I even had to sell the apartment that I had purchased for my mother. I remembered the day that I gave her the key, promising her that she'd never have to worry about a landlord again, and here I was, taking it all away from her. My brothers were furious with me because they thought I was just being stingy. I couldn't tell them about the Ponzi scheme; I was too ashamed to admit that we had been duped. The family was now right back where it had been when my father left: financially devastated and unsure of where we would all live. Instead of saving my mother and providing for her, I'd lost everything the same way Dad did.

Unlike my father, though, I was determined that I was going to get it all back. I promised that to Anna and I promised that to myself. Now, I just had to figure out how to do it.

I no longer believed that my place was in the corporate world. It had been devastating, but this latest call to adventure finally got through to me. I'd been chasing something—what I had believed to be my purpose—for my entire adult life. It had made me sick, it had made me sad, it had eroded my relationships, and it had made me hate myself. Now, finally, the pursuit of money and success had blown up my life around me.

I wasn't like Daniel Igali; I didn't have that clarity of purpose from a young age. If I'd ever had it, it had long ago been papered over by fear and trauma and the received "wisdom" of others. I had to have everything stripped away from me before I could really start to figure out what I wanted.

Our goal with The Way of the Quiet Warrior™ is to get our clients to that place without the pain and loss. We want to help people look within themselves and find that spark—however small it might be—of passion. We call this the "Definite Major Purpose" or the "DMP."

This phase is all about asking tough questions and helping people take real, honest looks at what is driving them. Many, many people are not being driven toward anything in their life. They are simply running *from* various things, whether it be failure or rejection or even their own traumatic memories. If your own goal is to get away from something, though, you can run wildly all over the place. You can even run in circles and you'll wind up getting nowhere at all.

And, as I discovered through painful experience, many of the things people most want to run away from are things that are deeply connected to them, things they cannot shake, no matter how hard they try. Trying to run from feelings of inadequacy or unhappiness or bad memories is like trying to flee a vicious dog . . . while holding his leash.

The entire concept of a Definite Major Purpose is to create something worth running *toward*. Daniel Igali didn't just want to leave Nigeria; he didn't just want to get away from his life. He had a specific, concrete goal that he wanted to achieve and he had a crystal-clear vision of the person he wanted to become: a champion.

The dissolution of the life I'd built—the life I had believed was my driving purpose—allowed me to finally see that the thing that really fulfilled me was the relationships I had and the ways in which I could help people. It wasn't money that had pushed me on for all those years, or even the adrenaline spike of success; it was that occasional feeling that I was being of service to others. With everything else stripped away, I could finally understand my own deepest motivations.

In addition to my overarching purpose, I also identified what I would eventually call "Personal Pivotal Needs," which are the smaller specific things that everyone requires to be truly happy. As our purpose burns within us, so do these individual desires and, if they go unmet, something always seems to be missing. These things, whether they're a desire to feel safe or obtain true health, are things that can drive our behavior, whether or not we acknowledge them.

For a long time, I had been suppressing many of my needs, and part of changing my life meant getting in touch with those needs all over again. This was where the motivation-based People Code and Character Code helped me a lot. Using that framework, I was able to correctly identify behaviors that were, unbeknownst to me, fueled by unmet needs.

Most motivations boil down to a need in one way or another, even if it's a somewhat roundabout way. Sometimes, the need-motivation link is very clear, e.g., Susan ate a doughnut because she needed to consume food to continue living. Sometimes, though, it's a little more esoteric than that. Perhaps Susan chose a doughnut and not a granola bar because she had a bad day and, when she was a little girl, her mother would buy her a doughnut whenever she had a bad day. In that case, the need she is meeting is a need for comfort, for soothing or a boost in happiness, and she could actually meet that need in a number of ways. She chose the doughnut because of a pattern that had been engrained in her since childhood.

People rarely think about their motivations, however, and if you asked Susan why she chose the doughnut, she would probably say something like, "It looked good." For her, that would be true because she did not care to examine her choices in the context of what she actually needed, versus the surface-level urge to have a treat.

That is why it is so important to identify our Personal Pivotal Needs, because it is only when we name and acknowledge those needs that we can examine our behavior and possibly find healthier ways to get what we need. In Phase Two, when we work on articulating our DMP, I also provide a list of common PPNs that clients can select from to complement their overarching purpose.

The very act of naming these things and putting them on paper can be powerful in terms of pushing us forward. The more we acknowledge our purposes, the more we "feed" them and the more powerful they become.

A DMP can sustain us through upsets and setbacks, it can move mountains and cross oceans, it can make an abused kid into a healer or an impoverished kid into an Olympian. It is a burning desire that encourages us to be better and faster and stronger every day, but we do have to nurture that fire within us or it will be smothered. In Phase Two of The Way of the Quiet Warrior™, we will help you find that flame and we will coax it to roaring life.

ROAD TRIP

The rules were simple and unalterable.

"Park down the next block. Don't get out of your car. Wait for me. If I don't come in fifteen minutes, I'm not coming." She always came, wearing the same plain black skirt and pressed blouse, and carrying a messenger bag like she was on her way to an appointment. She dressed the same way when she came to class, even if it was first thing in the morning. It was the only way, she said, that her parents would let her leave the house.

She never told me exactly what her parents believed she was doing when she left in the afternoon or evening dressed like an overgrown schoolgirl, but I could guess. Studying late, volunteering, an internship, something rigid immigrant parents could get behind. I understood that generally, if not her situation in particular. My parents were vagabonds who came from vagabonds; our blood was all mixed up and Canada was the third country they'd immigrated to since they had married.

Ellen's parents had come straight to Toronto from their home in Mainland China and they'd rooted themselves there. She still lived with them and her sister in the first apartment they'd rented in the city.

"They must be so proud of you," I told her once. Ellen was the fastest rising star in the business program we both attended. Except, perhaps, for me and my immigrant mother, who certainly never missed a chance to brag about her successful son.

Ellen just shook her head and said, "It's different." That was her favorite demurral. "It's different for me," "It's different for my family," "It's different for Chinese people." She never told me exactly *how* it was different or *why,* but being with Ellen was like moving through a dark room without a light; I was always feeling around for the barriers and the edges, the places where I could not pass.

"Go," was always the first thing she said when she slid into the passenger seat of my battered Plymouth Voyager. She never cared where we went, so long as it was away. When we were far from her home, out of her neighborhood entirely, she would wait until we were idling at a red light and then lean over to give me a chaste kiss on my temple.

"Thank you," she always said.

———

Ellen was the first girl I'd dated seriously (Ellen did everything seriously) and sometimes I wondered if this was the way it was supposed to be, having a girlfriend. But I had nothing with which to compare it.

Was a girlfriend supposed to get stiff and distant whenever you tried to so much as take her hand in public? Was she supposed to visibly bristle at the idea of taking her to see your mom? Was she only ever supposed to whisper when she called you on the phone, talking low and furtive like someone in a spy movie?

I met Ellen on my first day of class; she was in my econ seminar. The next day, I discovered that she was also in my statistics course and my communications for business majors course.

"We're on the same degree track," she said on the third day, sitting down beside me in our stats class. She didn't say anything else, but she sat next to me in all the other courses we shared as though it were the most natural thing in the world, as though we were already part of a team.

When I asked her if she'd like to study with me at the library, she nodded at me in a slightly bewildered way, as though she had already taken my offer as a given. We stayed at the library for seven hours that first day, long into the night. We studied for the first three and then we just talked, complaining about the rich kids in the program who slouched in the far-back seats, still smelling like last night's party. We laughed about the idea of being so lucky as to attend this university and then wasting the opportunity boozing and slacking off.

It was the first time I heard her laugh. It was a good laugh.

We made a kind of pact then, if not in so many words. We were going to be different than the rich kids, the white kids whose parents and grandparents had been born here, the ones who napped through classes like a top-flight education was their birthright. We were going to outwork, out-study, and outwit them, and we were going to lap them in every one of our courses.

I thought (maybe I flattered myself) that I was a little bit smarter than Ellen but I had never met anyone with a more capacious or exacting mind than she. She would go over and over our textbook until she could recite it, she would redo stats problems until they were engraved on both of our brains. I wondered, sometimes, if she even needed to do all these practice drills. We were both getting top marks, far outstripping our classmates and the material didn't feel that challenging to me. When I told her this, however, she just clucked her tongue at me.

"The better we do in these courses, the sooner we can move on, the sooner we can graduate, the sooner we can attract attention from the good graduate programs."

Ellen had a plan for her future. Or rather, a lot of little plans that all went the same place: out, away, gone. *Go.*

We had been dating for nearly two months when I found out she was still only seventeen. I was barely nineteen myself, but still, this information threw me.

"I completed secondary in three years," she told me. "There was no need to wait."

She told me the same thing when she plopped down a newspaper in front of me, all of the listings for one-bedroom apartments circled in green ink.

"I will get a job," she said, "in three months when I turn eighteen. These are the ones we can afford."

I looked at the paper but couldn't seem to focus on the actual words. All I saw was a forest of green circles.

"I don't know if I'm . . . ready for that," I managed finally. My plan (in the limited way that I had a plan) was to continue living with my mother and my sister until I finished my undergraduate degree. It was the cheapest and most sensible option, something I would have imagined Ellen would appreciate.

"But you love me, don't you?" she asked, giving me that same bewildered look that she'd had the first time I asked her to study with me. In her head, this step was not only natural, but also inevitable, and my hesitance was inexplicable to her.

Before I could answer, she said, "I love *you*." She said it the same way she announced the answer to a test question or confirmed the date of an appointment: simple, factual, immutable. If she had gushed or cried or let her voice quiver, I might not have been so struck by it but no one had ever told me they loved me before. It was not the kind of thing we said in our family and none of the girls I'd pined for in high school had given me a second glance, let alone their heart. And here was Ellen, talking about her love for me like it was gravity or oxygen or water, just one fact of the world that should be obvious to anyone with eyes.

"I love you too," I said. And, in that moment, it was true.

———

Julienne was technically my twin but it had been years since I'd referred to her that way. "Sister" was a better, more accurate description of our relationship. When someone hears "twin," they think *two halves of a whole,* but Julienne wasn't any part of me and I don't think she'd want me to make up a part of her either.

We didn't look alike. I was short and, when I was younger, plump like Mom, and Julienne was tall and leggy like Dad. She had Dad's quick smile, as well, and his fall of dark hair. People loved her easily and immediately, just like he did.

Mom and I were more of an acquired taste: quieter, less given to smiling in general. Julienne was frequently impatient with the both of us.

"Stop *pitying* yourself," she would say. "The past is the past." For her, maybe that was the truth. For me, the past was every day. Every day when Dad was conspicuously absent, every day when I came home to the cramped two-bedroom apartment that was just about all we could afford as we steadily paid down the ocean of debt that was my father's only legacy. The past was crushing me.

"That's crazy," Julienne said flatly when I told her about Ellen's plan. She already thought Ellen was "some kind of weirdo" because she kept finding reasons not to come out to the house and meet my family. For the first month we were dating, Julienne had even insinuated that I'd made Ellen up, created a fake girlfriend to make Mom feel better about me being all alone at school. By now, she believed Ellen was real, but clearly thought that something was wrong with her—the insinuation being that there would have to be if Ellen could love *me*.

I looked to Mom, usually my backup in just about everything, but her face was hesitant and I could tell that she didn't think Julienne was entirely wrong.

"She seems very . . . motivated," Mom said finally, diplomatically.

"She loves me," I insisted, "and she wants us to be together."

"She's probably trying to get her hooks into you," Julienne said with a totally unearned air of authority. "You said she's from Mainland China, right?"

"Her *parents* are—"

"Whatever. Same difference. You know how they are. They're basically like peasants back home and then they come here and try to snag a rich, white guy to bankroll their lifestyle."

I gestured around the kitchen, the linoleum that bubbled up and stuck to our bare feet when we walked on it, the faucet that dribbled a constant stream of grayish water from the loose base, the broken sliding glass door that hadn't been fixed the entire time we'd lived there.

"I'm not rich," I said, "or white." Mom's dad was white but, somehow, it wasn't the 25 percent Caucasian in me that people noticed first.

"You're close enough to both for someone who grew up starving on a rice farm or wherever," Julienne sniffed.

"She was born in Toronto!"

"I'm just saying! You've gotta look out for yourself. Next thing you know, she's gonna try to get pregnant and then you'll really be on the hook."

I decided not to inform Julienne that pregnancy was very unlikely, considering the fact that Ellen and I hadn't done more than kiss. "I don't do that," Ellen had said stiffly when I'd broached the subject once and I couldn't tell if it was religious or just personal, but I could tell that she didn't want to talk about it. So I didn't.

Instead, I rolled my eyes. "Gee, I can't imagine why she doesn't want to meet the two of you."

———————

"My parents will meet you," Ellen said and I heard a little tremor in her voice. That hadn't been the reason I was reluctant to move in with her but I had to admit that the idea made me feel good. Practically speaking, asking someone to share an apartment with you was a much more significant relationship step than meeting the parents but Ellen had always been so circumspect about her family. This invitation *felt* like something big, something important.

"You can come for dinner on Friday," she said. "You should bring a gift. They will not take it at first, but you must insist. Flowers are good. Don't bring food." She paused then and her face was hesitant. "I've told them you're my . . . friend."

I could tell from the way she said it that she didn't mean "special friend," but that her parents did not know about our relationship. This wasn't exactly a surprise to me, though she had never explicitly said as much.

"They don't mind your having a male friend?"

Ellen looked down and away. It was rare that she would refuse to meet my eyes.

"I have to go slowly with them," she said. "Like inching into cold water. First, they'll meet you as a friend. Then, we'll see. When the time comes," she raised her head to look directly at me again, "what they say and what they do will not stop me." It felt like a promise, not just to me, but also to herself.

Ellen swallowed hard.

"Before you go," she said, "there are some things I have to tell you about my family."

It wasn't much different from any other time I'd picked her up, at least at first. She asked me to park down the block in the same place I always parked and she asked me to wait for her. She was even wearing the same black skirt and white blouse when she came out to fetch me.

"You told them I was coming, right?" I asked her again when she came out, taking me by the hand and leading me up the sidewalk.

"Yes. But we must be careful. Slow." Her voice was tight and her face was eerily blank, as though it had been patiently scrubbed of all emotion. A small woman whom I took to be her mother met us at the door, smiling and nodding her head at me like I'd said something worth agreeing with.

Ellen didn't look much like her mother. She looked a lot like the little girl I saw watching silently from the apartment's living room, however. Already seated at the dining room table and looking profoundly unwilling to move was a jowly older man, Ellen's father.

Ellen made the introductions but I only parsed the occasional word. It was like someone was crinkling up plastic bottles right next to my ear. Beside me, Ellen felt like a spring compressed down into a solid muscle but practically vibrating with repressed kinetic energy. I couldn't remember a time in my life when I had been less comfortable in my own body.

Her mother spoke in slightly awkward, accented English. She sounded as though she had practiced some of her sentences in large chunks. Periodically, she would break off into Mandarin to say something to her husband or one of the girls. Ellen's younger sister answered her in sullen English while her father responded only with grunts or opaque facial expressions.

"Come, sit and eat," she said cheerfully, taking my arm and pulling me toward the dining room table, which had indeed been set with a number of small enamel pots, steam oozing out of them.

I took a seat next to Ellen and across from the younger girl. She gave me a look of bored appraisal that would not have been out of place on the faces of the girls I had known in high school. She didn't appear to have any of Ellen's intensity or her strangeness. She seemed . . . normal, like some foreign-exchange student from the land of well-adjusted people.

———————

"He never touched my little sister," she told me, sitting quietly in the library parking lot in my car. "I made sure of that. I told him if he ever put his hands on her, I would cut my throat. I would do it in a big way; I would make it obvious. Everyone would see what his daughter had done and he would never recover from that." She seemed almost proud of herself. She wasn't smiling but she had that look on her face like she might smile.

"He started with me when I was—" The sentence got stuck in her throat and came out sounding strangled. "—much younger than she is now. So if he was going to do it to her, I think he would have by now. So I think I scared him." Something like doubt had crept into her voice. I watched her hands as she spoke; she massaged her knuckles and pulled nervously at her fingers.

"Does your mother know?" I asked.

"My mom . . . tries her hardest not to know."

———————

Ellen's mother had prepared a truly heroic amount of food. Plates of crispy pork belly and beef tongue in sauce, fat white steam buns and little crinkled dumplings with cloudy skin that exposed the shrimp and vegetables inside.

"*Siu mai,*" Ellen frowned. "Shrimp is BaBa's favorite."

It was a little overwhelming and Ellen's mother paid special attention to my plate, heaping food upon it until I had four or five times the amount I could have comfortably eaten.

Ellen's mother moved strangely, almost compulsively, smiling and laughing at what seemed to be random moments. Occasionally, her father would spit out something in Chinese, scorn clear on his face, and her mother's expression would falter, but she always bounced back. She always settled back into that strange, detached smile.

Ellen had warned me that while her father could speak English fluently, he would probably choose not to. "His accent is worse than my mother's. He's sensitive about it." She did not warn me, however, about how his eyes would glide right over me as though I were not there at all or how he would not so much as greet me when I sat down.

I wondered if he was waiting for me to introduce myself forcefully. I wondered if that was the sort of thing I was supposed to do, as a man. I wondered but I did nothing; instead, I tried to eat, though everything tasted the same: like nothingness. All I felt was the different temperature and weight of each bite, nothing of the flavor.

I supposed, though, that whatever Ellen's father thought a man was or should be, I wanted to be the exact opposite. It was for the best, I thought, that he hadn't tried to shake my hand. The thought of touching him was repellant.

Ellen's mother had supplied me both with a fork and with chopsticks and I selected the fork, which made her nod approvingly.

"I didn't know what you want. Ellen told me you were—" and then she said something in Mandarin that I couldn't understand but it sounded like it ended with "acin" or "a-sin." Apparently, whatever it was, it wasn't what she had intended to say because she immediately shut her mouth and looked down at the tablecloth awkwardly.

Ellen said something to her in Chinese, pointed and rebuking, and her mother nodded. Then, her father burst forth with a flurry of words, clearly angry. Across from me, Ellen's younger sister rolled her eyes.

———————

"It's a . . . rude word," she told me afterward as she walked me back to my car, "for an Indian person. She shouldn't have said it."

"But I'm not Indian," I protested. "Just my dad was."

And only barely, at that. He had been born in London and he only went to India once as a young boy. He didn't even really remember the trip.

"You're Indian enough for them," Ellen sighed. "They think all Indian people are poor and dirty and . . . untrustworthy." She sounded ashamed as she said it and I thought about Julienne cautioning me against Mainland Chinese women. I wondered what my father would have said, if he were alive to see me with Ellen. Would he have disliked and distrusted her based on the colour of her skin?

"That's stupid," I said and Ellen nodded.

"It is stupid but they will disown me over it."

I looked at her, startled, and to my surprise, Ellen laughed.

"Don't worry," she said. "One way or another, I was always going to cut them out. I've known that for a long time now."

"So . . . this dinner wasn't about getting them to like me?"

By then, we were standing beside my parked car and I was fiddling with my keys restlessly, sure that I should be doing something but unsure of exactly what.

"They'll never like you," Ellen said and she seemed to have no notion of the idea that this statement might hurt me. Her voice was brisk and clean, the way it always was when she was instructing me or apprising me of a new plan. "But there are still things you have to do in a Chinese family and now we have done them. When they reject me, it will be their choice, not mine."

———————

After the meal, I half expected Ellen's father to pull me aside for the sort of man-to-man chats that I imagined boyfriends had with fathers all the time. So, when the man actually did stand up and push his chair back, I stood up almost automatically. Ellen's father looked and me, frowning slightly, and I realized that it was not me whom he wanted to speak to in private.

Ellen gave my hand a squeeze that I think she meant to be comforting but her hand was quivering slightly and she squeezed too hard, desperately and painfully. She left me at the table with her endlessly smiling mother and her sister who was idly drawing designs in the remains of her meal with one chopstick.

I could hear them in the kitchen. Ellen's father was making no attempt to talk softly, though Ellen's responses were just a low murmur. I couldn't understand what he was saying, but the women at the table could. Ellen's sister just scowled while her mother bustled around, clearing dishes from the table and muttering what I took to be apologies under her breath.

Ellen came out of the kitchen like a bullet from a gun, stopping only briefly at the table to pull me to my feet. She didn't even say good-bye to her family as she led the two of us to front door. I scrambled to put my shoes back on while she stood there, impatient in almost an alarmed way, looking back at the table and out the front window like we were being chased by wild dogs or enemy soldiers.

"Are you OK?"

"I don't want to be here anymore."

"I know."

———————

It was the first time I'd seen her cry, in the passenger seat of the Voyager in the nearly abandoned library parking lot. She curled herself up against the seat back, driving her elbows into her knees. She allowed her hair to fall over her face so I could not see her tears, but I could hear them.

"I've never told that to anyone," she sobbed. "I've never . . . said it out loud. What he did to me."

I wanted to say something. It felt like I should say something, like someone should say something. This moment could not just hang there, unmarked.

Before I could, though, she sat up and pushed the hair out of her face. She was red, from the skin just above her eyebrows to her lips, which looked shiny and abraded. "I've never trusted anyone enough before you. I'll never trust anyone like this again."

She reached out, her hand clasping mine almost like a claw.

"You have to stay with me," she said. "I won't make it if you don't."

As soon as we left the apartment building and shut the door behind us, Ellen's body transformed. Her movements became loose and easy, she walked slowly and without the fierce purpose I had seen inside. Her face seemed to both brighten and lift.

"I have to go back tonight. But soon, I won't." She smiled at me and I struggled to smile back. "Do you know that, when I was little, I used to tell my mother that I would never get married?"

As we walked, I looked into the windows on either side of the street, I peered into the cracks where the curtains didn't quite meet, trying to make out something inside. Maybe a family, maybe a couple, maybe an empty room.

"When I imagined being an adult, I always imagined that I was alone," Ellen continued, her voice uncharacteristically soft. "I thought that was my fate in life. But now I know that I was wrong."

She looked up at me and I wanted nothing more than to look back at her but I couldn't. I was afraid, I think, of what she would see if I did.

"Now I know that you are my fate."

"And I just sat there. Like a lump. Three feet away from him. I wanted to . . . do something."

Mom gave me a questioning look. She was wondering, just like I was, what I could have done. Hit Ellen's father? Called the police? Pick Ellen up and whisk her away? But Ellen was already doing a pretty good job of whisking herself away, and me along with her.

"Honey, you can't stay with this girl." Mom reached out and tried to take my hands but I pulled them away, horrified. That was the kind of thing that I'd expect to hear from Julienne. Look out for number one; that was her ethos. But Mom and I had always understood one another. Of all the people in my world, I thought my mother would understand feeling obligated to help someone who needed a seemingly unending amount of help.

"I can't *leave her*." I could almost taste the words in my mouth, like food that had gone off.

"Because you love her?"

"Because I love her," I said firmly but I could see in her face that she didn't entirely believe me. I *did* love Ellen, or at least I was pretty sure I did. But I was definitely sure that she loved me and needed me, and walking away from people who need you isn't something good people do. Mom should know that by now. I had stayed here, after all, after the money had run out and no one else would take care of her and Julienne. She had to know what kind of person I was. She had to know how I was different from *him*.

"You can't undo all the hurt that has been done to her," Mom said. "You can't fix her inside," she touched her own chest in the place where her heart was, "not by yourself."

"We'll get help." I said it easily though I knew that Ellen would not go willingly into anything that had a whiff of therapy about it. We had time, though. We had the rest of our lives to recover from the first two decades.

"I can't stop you." I hated that look on her face, that tone in her voice. I knew it well; it was the same one she got whenever Dad insisted that he was only going to have *one* drink, that he was only going out for *one* hour. It was a look and a tone that meant she hated what he was doing down to her bones but she felt helpless in the face of his much stronger will.

I didn't like that, her putting him and me in the same category in her head, however temporarily, and so I was angry when I answered her.

"No, you can't stop me! And I can't figure out why you would want to!"

She looked stricken and I immediately felt bad.

"I'm not telling you to be cruel."

"No, no. I know you're not."

This time, I was the one to reach out for her hand.

———————

Julienne helped me pack. Mom must have told her about our conversation, but she didn't say anything about it. Instead, she nattered on about her waitressing job and the stray cat she'd found who was going to have kittens. Sometimes Julienne could be pretty OK, as sisters go.

She only raised the issue once, and obliquely at that.

"All set?" she asked me after we had loaded the last of the boxes into the Voyager. She could have just been talking about having everything packed but I could tell by the look on her face that she wasn't.

"Gotta be," I said and I could have been talking about the boxes too. But I wasn't.

When you have a twin, people love to tell you stories about twins and something I had often heard was how sometimes sets of twins will develop their own special language that they only use with one another. Julienne and I had never bothered with that (some might say Julienne had yet to fully master English) but I wondered now if this wasn't a mild form of that, me looking at her and knowing without her saying that she was questioning my decision and her looking at me and knowing that I was making the only choice that I could.

She must have understood because she gave me a hug and that was something she almost never did.

"You know," she said, close to my ear, "it's not enough just to know who you *don't* want to be."

"OK, Oprah," I said, pulling away from her and rolling my eyes.

"Get out here," Julienne grinned in response, "so I can turn the room into a karate dojo or something."

But I thought about her words as I got behind the wheel and buckled my seatbelt, and I kept thinking about them as I drove everything I owned over to the modest one-bedroom Ellen had leased for the two of us. *It's not enough just to know who you* don't *want to be.* And I thought, too, about my strange, fragile, serious girlfriend in the passenger seat begging me to just *go* and take her to an unknown destination that had to be better if only by virtue of not being here. Sometimes I would just drive her around in circles, burning gas and getting nowhere but she never seemed to mind.

I was thinking so hard, I almost drove right past the apartment complex. I'd almost missed my destination; how stupid would that have been?

3 PHASE THREE
THE
PATH

What is the secret to success?

I t may not have felt like it in the midst of the chaos and loss from our investment disaster, but I was a lucky man. I thought of myself as having lost everything but, in reality, my most powerful assets were still there. For one thing, I still had myself, all of my flaws and virtues intact. I was healthy and young and I had my years of experience and my drive to succeed. Even more importantly, though, I had Anna.

Many other people in her position would have immediately pushed me to get back into the corporate world and start rebuilding our nest egg. No one would have blamed her if she'd told me to put my search for purpose on hold and return to what I knew, but Anna didn't do any of that. Instead, she did something that was revolutionary for me: she trusted me.

For another person, this might not have been so remarkable—husbands and wives should trust one another, after all—but for someone like me, who had spent years essentially mistrusting myself, denying my instincts and my emotions, it was incredible. Anna's faith in me was a gift and I was determined to honour that gift and make sure that she never regretted giving it to me.

The house was our largest asset so, naturally, that was one of the first things to go when we had to create liquid cash in a hurry. For a while, we rented a house while we got our bearings but once we settled our debts and got our heads above water, we decided to take the remainder of our money and put it into a property in a resort community. This was a place we knew well; we'd spent vacations there since shortly after we were married. Our kids had grown up spending summers there and many of our happiest family memories were set against the backdrop of that place. For all those reasons, Anna and I had always talked about relocating there permanently. That was something for the future, after the kids had gone off to college and we had both retired; we were going to build our dream house. After everything we had been through, though, the idea of putting off our dreams and hopes no longer seemed appealing.

I took the same approach to my career, diving right in and working as hard as I could to find that true avocation that would fulfill me and drive me. Because I wasn't sure exactly what I wanted to do, I was a little like an indecisive customer at an ice cream shop: I had to try a little bit of everything. I took a real estate broker course, which wound up leading me to investigate Tony Robbins and his "Date with Destiny" course down in Florida, where I learned how to name and map my values. This course really helped me to look past the narratives I'd developed about my life and situation, and gave me a real, honest glimpse of the concepts that had been ruling my life: self-pity, constant feeling of failure, anxiety, sadness, rejection.

This was revolutionary for me and it allowed me to really think for the first time about what values I *wanted* to prioritize in my life, not simply the forces that I had allowed to shape me from childhood on. I was essentially rewiring myself, changing all my thought patterns and instincts from the ground up, and it was amazing. This was when I discovered that I could actually use my awful childhood as a tool to help others like me. I could take a bad situation and turn it into a genuine gift.

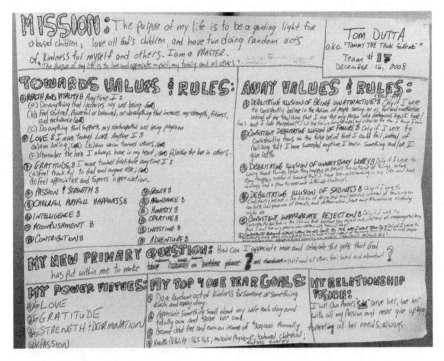

This was the chart I created with Tony Robbins. It shows my old and new values…it was the point in my life that I rewired my thinking to change my old story. The practice helped cement my purpose. I took a photo of it.

That was when I started to get a real sense of what my true purpose is: I want to reach out to people like me. People who are living with unprocessed trauma, people who are desperate and trapped and don't know how to get out of the prisons they have made for themselves. I want to show others the escape hatch I had found.

I found myself thinking specifically of all the people I'd met in the corporate sector and the patterns of behavior that I'd seen so often. Jobs in the corporate world can be incredibly rewarding and interesting but it is a high-stress world and the stress never really lets up. There are a few rare individuals who thrive on an atmosphere of constant challenge, but far, far more common are people like me, people who are struggling but pretending to be fine on the outside. Success is incredible and thrilling but that feeling is often momentary and fleeting—true happiness can last a lifetime. I have seen so much conflict and miscommunication and failure because people don't have a real sense of themselves and what would actually make them happy.

The more I thought about this, the more engaged I became. I continued my adventure, spending hours studying new concepts, new tools for managing interpersonal relationships and understanding how trauma actually physically impacts our brain. The more I learned, the more sense it made. I found out that when we have conflict or injury, it can actually change the pathways in our brains and that is why it can be so incredibly hard to break out of destructive patterns; those patterns actually feel right and natural to our brains.

This explained so much of what I had seen in my career when I would spend weeks or months working with someone and helping her build new communication and conflict-resolution skills and seeing a true understanding in her, only to find that, after a few months, she had returned to her old, dysfunctional ways. She knew it wasn't good, but it felt *right*. Comfortable and familiar, even soothing in a strange way. It explained why my family members and I missed my father after he'd left us: the cycle of abuse was not a positive thing in any way but it was something that had been ingrained in us after years and years of repetition. Without that familiar circuit of tension, eruption, contrition, and a brief honeymoon phase before it all began again, we didn't quite know what to do with ourselves. For as long as my brothers and I could remember, that had been the structure of our lives. It was no wonder that we had each, in our separate ways, sought out living situations that provided that same sort of stress and trauma. We craved it; our father had inculcated an addiction within us, just like his addiction to alcohol.

It was around this time that I first stumbled upon the work of Joseph Campbell, which immediately resonated with me. One idea that I immediately latched onto was Campbell's assertion that the ultimate end to the Hero's Journey wasn't accomplishing the task he or she had set out to complete, but bringing a greater knowledge or wisdom (what Campbell calls the Hero's "boon") back to the larger ordinary world. That was what I wanted to be, but it was even more than a want; it was a calling. I had found something, and it had taken years of suffering and striving, and it felt vital and important that I bring it to others. This was the burning, undeniable purpose that Napoleon Hill talks about.

Once I had that sense of purpose, however, I quickly realized that a purpose is only the beginning. If only 5 percent of people ever truly know their purpose in life, it is an even smaller percent of people who are actually able to *realize* that purpose. It's incredibly difficult for people to make *any* goal a reality, let alone a large, complex one. Even more difficult is getting our thoughts and feelings to work toward our goals instead of against them. This is a huge topic both in science and in life, and many people just can't get their head around it. That limitation, I believe, leads to a lot of failure and frustration in both life and work.

I began to think of this process as sort of like a jigsaw puzzle. When you're putting together a puzzle, it's good to have that picture that comes on the box (many people might argue that it is necessary, in fact), but knowing what the final image should look like won't make the pieces just fall into place.

I had a lot of pieces and a clear image of what my final result should be and now I had to do the patient work of putting all the pieces together. The puzzle metaphor works for me on another level too, though, because putting together a puzzle is essentially about changing your way of seeing. You look at the picture on the box and you know that you're creating a barn next to a river and suddenly, those pieces aren't just bits of red or blue cardboard, they are the uppermost corner of the barn or the edge of the river with some rushes. The pieces themselves have not changed, but you've had to figure out how to see them. It is only then that you can make sense of the puzzle as a whole.

The concepts of seeing and vision are huge in the corporate world. I had been hearing about making visions a reality, manifesting goals, visualizing the future in seminars and workshops for years, so I was very familiar with the idea that making things happen is a process that starts with your mind's eye. Until I really dug into the research, however, I had never truly realized how powerful the subconscious mind is and how much it contributes to our success or failure.

For example, consider the game of golf. Great golfers use visualization to help them win. If you are standing on a golf course preparing to swing and you look down the green, what do you see? Well, if you are the average unskilled player, you probably see lots of things: the bunkers on the right, the water to the left, the birds flying overhead, and the people standing around watching you, among countless other details great and small. Now, if you were Tiger Woods in his prime and you looked down that same green, you would see one thing and one thing only: success. You would have such a strong visualization of your shot sinking into the hole that it would drive out any and all other distractions. Elite players might as well be performing in an isolation tank for all the attention they pay to the crowds and the landscape and all the features of daily life that preoccupy so many of us.

I learned to play golf as a young child. My father taught me and, as with most of his lessons, it was reinforced with pain and fear. He used violence to instruct me, forcing my body into the correct posture and holding me there with his hand clamped down on my skull until I could feel a dull, pounding ache in my skull.

He had a set of old-fashioned wooden clubs and I still remember being made to stand perfectly still while he swung them directly at my face. If I flinched, I would be punished and while this was ostensibly to help me develop calm and fearlessness, I was always aware of how my dad seemed to thrive on my fear and how provoking it seemed to make him feel powerful and in control. The last thing my dad wanted, really, was a fearless son.

I got reasonably good at golf; partially, it was because I knew I would be punished for failing to absorb Dad's "lessons" and partially, because—even though I knew it was impossible—I wanted to make him happy. As an adult, I kept up the practice. Golf is a very popular sport in the corporate world, so I had plenty of opportunities to keep up my skills. I rarely thought about my father during those games, though I automatically incorporated his edicts about how to swing, how to hold my head and my hips. They were muscle memory by that point, like many of the other things he had taught me.

Imagine my surprise, then, when I was preparing to play a round of golf with some potential clients one afternoon and discovered that I was profoundly, inexplicably terrified of the idea of going out on the course. I couldn't understand it; I knew those men. I'd played golf hundreds of times before. I was anticipating a positive interaction overall, and yet I was deeply, viscerally afraid. I was having something like a panic attack, and not knowing why it was happening didn't make the fear any less real.

I eventually had to call my golfing partners and tell them that I was too sick to play. This was something that I almost never did—I'd never been one for missing appointments—and it must have seemed unusual and inconvenient to them, but I couldn't think of what else to do. As it was, I spent the rest of the day cloistered in my hotel room, trying to calm myself back down.

It was some time before I figured out what had happened to me that day: something about that day, that course, those men, the game of golf itself had sparked something deep in my mind, something I thought I'd put to rest years ago. It wasn't rational or logical and it had nothing to do with the situation I was actually in. I had been transported—in my mind, at least—back to my childhood. I was a scared kid all over again, desperately wanting to avoid going out onto the green and experiencing my father's wrath.

I had actually become a decent golfer over the years; I'd even gone to the WGC-American Express Championship in Atlanta, Georgia, with my clients on a VIP trip, following Tiger Woods, Vijay Singh (a Fijian golfer and a family fave), K. J. Choi, and Canadian Mike Weir—an incredible foursome. As Tony Robbins helped me discover years later, however, two of the biggest human fears are failure and not being loved enough. I had somehow developed a fear that I would be judged and derided out on the golf course and that fear had shut me down entirely.

That is the power of the subconscious mind; it can make you a champion or it can make you a wreck. I was discovering, though, that the subconscious mind is not a master, but a tool. With the proper techniques and knowledge, you can change the deep-seated patterns in your life and replace them with new, healthier patterns.

The subconscious mind is vast and deep. If you think of the entire mind as an iceberg, our conscious mind is the tip, visible, knowable, and the smallest part of the whole. The subconscious mind is the ice underneath, the 90 percent that is out of sight. Your subconscious mind is always working, whirring away—noticing things and processing data—all while your conscious mind thinks about larger things, like work and family and the physical actions you are currently performing. When you are driving your car, for example, you may think that your mind is completely absorbed with the business of getting from point A to point B. Somewhere deep in your subconscious, however, your brain is noting things like the telephone poles you're passing, the car behind you that is just edging into your blind spot, the almost imperceptible noise that the air conditioner is making. All of these things are being noted and logged and filed away somewhere in your brain.

The problem is that a lot of things that happen to, or around, us are negative things. The older we get, the more details and memories are stored in our subconscious mind and, naturally, the more negative things are stored there as well. I think of these negative ideas and thought patterns as "weeds" in our subconscious because they can choke out and replace the healthy thoughts. We are the guardians at the gate and the subconscious mind believes what you teach it, even if what you are teaching it doesn't make sense. If I truly believe an orange is black and I reinforce that belief, I will begin to see black oranges. At some point in my life, for example, the idea that golf equals pain became embedded deep in my subconscious mind, and that thought became so strong that it was able to overwhelm my rational conscious mind in a negative way. The more of these "weeds" that spring up, the harder it is to think creatively or freely.

We are the masters of our own gardens, though, and we can choose to plant certain seeds, just like we can choose to uproot the weeds. For The Way of the Quiet Warrior™ specifically, one thing we want to do is to plant our purpose in our subconscious mind. We want to root it deeply and reinforce it frequently so it can blossom there and we can begin manifesting the future we want for ourselves.

We start with what I have often seen called a "vision board." It is basically just a place where you can articulate your purpose in both words and images. I prefer to call them "movie boards" because I find that mine are evolving; they are in motion. Just as a screenwriter might create a storyboard for a movie, I've created a storyboard for my life.

My visual "movie" board that I created for my first DMP

I also encourage my clients to write down their Definite Major Purpose (DMP) and actually make an audio recording of it. It doesn't have to be long, three to five minutes is plenty for most people, but I find that it's good to have this information in as many formats as you can manage. Our goal with all of this is to bombard our mind with this purpose. To that end, I post copies of my board all around my house: in the bedroom, the bathroom, the kitchen, and the office. It's even the wallpaper image on my computer and phone. I look at my purpose when I'm brushing my teeth or preparing dinner or getting ready to go to sleep. It might look a little weird to outsiders but this practice means that my subconscious mind is almost always exposed to these ideas. Just as my father embedded toxic things in my mind through sheer repetition, I can now use a similar tactic to embed positive ideas.

Returning to an idea over and over again (especially a positive idea) can actually be a comfort as you move through difficult times in your journey. For me, having the audio version of my movie board was invaluable. It meant that, wherever I went, I still had this tether to my ultimate goal. There were times in those early days when I had a setback or just felt that familiar anxiety creeping back in, and, in those moments, I would find a private place to listen to my recording. I even pulled my car off to the side of the road once to listen. Reinforcing those hopeful, purpose-driven thought patterns soothed me and encouraged me and allowed me to keep fighting against the challenges I faced.

Embedding your purpose in your subconscious mind is about more than just emotions, though, it also has a very practical value. Have you ever noticed that when you buy a new car, you suddenly start to notice other cars of the same make and model everywhere you go? That's not an uncommon experience and, in fact, there's even a term for it, the Baader-Meinhof phenomenon (or the slightly less Germanic-sounding "frequency illusion"). Our brains are great at spotting patterns; they are so great, in fact, that they will sometimes create patterns where none exist. That's why people see faces on the moon or religious figures in slices of toast, and that's why, when you just purchased a red truck, you suddenly see red trucks everywhere you look. The actual number of red trucks on the road has not changed; you have simply primed your brain to look for the ones that are there.

These general human tendencies can be troublesome; they can cause us to act in opposition to reason and logic, but if used correctly, they can also be enormously helpful. If you expose your subconscious mind to your purpose over and over again, your mind will begin looking for connections in the world around you. It will do this without needing direction from your conscious mind at all. Each one of us has what amounts to an incredibly powerful pattern-matching computer at our disposal; all we have to do is feed it the right information and let it work.

For example, when I was working overtime as a CEO trying to launch a new company, I knew vaguely in the back of my mind that my health was not good. When I wasn't working or traveling for work (not very often), I was sleeping, fighting against a fatigue that never seemed to relent. I was overweight and my doctor gave me medication to manage my spiking cholesterol. I never exercised, I ate poorly and drank with clients, and I started developing muscle aches that could only be relieved by hours in a hot tub. I was either tired or in pain—often both—nearly all the time.

Still, I didn't think I had time to deal with this. I was in my thirties and feeling about sixty, but I thought I had more important things to deal with. Finally, my body forced me to deal with it by nearly giving out during a particularly scary episode. I went in to see my doctor and she told me that I had to get off my cholesterol medication. Apparently, some people were experiencing side effects with it, including muscle deterioration. She thought that was what was causing my constant pain.

Even worse, as the muscle fibers broke down, tissue could actually enter my bloodstream and cause embolisms or even strokes. The event I had experienced was sort of a milder pre-stroke but I had no desire to go through the real thing!

Alarmed, I immediately stopped taking that drug and refused others (which, I discovered, contained slightly different formulations of the same active ingredients). I had no idea what to do but I knew that I couldn't keep doing what I had been. I got in my car and left the doctor's office confused and worried, hoping for some different pathway to open up to me.

I was thinking obsessively about health and wellness and how to achieve it, and that's when my brain plucked out a few key words from a radio commercial, I half heard as I was flicking through the dial. Immediately, I scrolled back to the station, which was airing an advertisement for a naturopathic clinic that provided nontraditional healing.

I drove there directly.

As soon as I met Dr. Talib, I felt confident that I'd made the right decision. She examined me and found a number of areas of concern, including my adrenal glands, my liver, and my gallbladder. After examining me and listening to my history, she told me that I had a tough row to hoe, genetically speaking, but that she believed she could help me.

After six months with Dr. Talib, I had no symptoms, no ongoing issues. Eventually, I got more serious about True Health and began changing my eating and exercise plans, and the more I got into these concepts, the more I saw how people around me could really benefit from a different approach to health.

Just as addressing my own emotional issues led to me seeing a lot of the same patterns in others, fixing my physical issues opened my eyes to just how many people in high-powered leadership positions are living the same kind of unhealthy—frankly, *deadly*—lifestyle I had been.

This idea eventually gave rise to the "Optimal Health KREATOR " component of The Way of the Quiet Warrior™, in which we create a program specifically designed to work for busy people with demanding jobs. True Health is an important component of my overall DMP (helping others break away from toxic patterns), but it was not something that I would have initially included. Only after I made health a regular component of my own life was I able to see the pattern of poor physical health connecting with poor emotional health, diminished performance at work, and a lack of joy at home. That is the power of pattern spotting, if we allow our brains to do that work.

The subconscious is the key to manifesting our purpose in this life, so I quickly realized that I had to find better ways to understand and manipulate my subconscious mind. To that end, I began to experiment with various exercises designed to allow you to get more of a "direct line" to your subconscious. The simplest of these (and one of my favorites) is called a "Sit and Think." Just as the name implies, all you need to do this exercise is a quiet place to be alone and your own brain.

I started with something that was deceptively simple. The task was to pick a spot on the wall and focus on it, truly focus, for five minutes. I was not allowed to let my mind wander into other avenues. If I had an itch on my nose, I couldn't scratch it. If I smelled dinner cooking in the next room, I could not imagine what it might be. It was much, much harder than I was expecting it to be. I actually had to work up to the full five minutes because I found it nearly impossible to control my racing mind.

Eventually, though, I was able to clear away all the "noise" and really hone in on this point-specific piece of wall. It made me so aware of the thousands upon thousands of thoughts that flit through our minds on a daily basis and it gave me a concrete way to press pause on some of those thoughts and really apply my full attention to just one thing—even if that one thing was a blank wall.

The next step in the process was to actually manifest something in my mind, to take that focus I had practiced and apply it to creating a fully realized vision of something that wasn't physically in the room with me. I was "building" something in my mind and I worked my way up from simple objects to an entire battleship, Navy sailors included.

The next step was to take that painstakingly visualized battleship and tear it down—or rather, to reverse engineer it. So I started with my now-familiar image of an imposing battleship, a floating fortress with flags and gun turrets and men in crisp uniforms moving like distant ants on the top decks. Then, slowly, I began to reverse engineer the ship in my mind. Like a film being played backward, I pictured the turrets being removed, the component parts being stripped away, leaving just a skeleton of a watercraft until even that, too, is gone. Then I took it a step further; I imagined molten streams of steel being moved and manipulated, men working with thick gloves and intense protective gear. The more I practiced this exercise, the further back I went. I imagined workers deep under the earth, pulling ore from the ground and piling it into huge mining carts. It was so vivid to me that I could see the dirt on their faces and the shimmering bits of debris in the lights from their headlamps.

I practiced making and unmaking this battleship until it became like second nature to me. I could control my thoughts, control my focus, I could keep intrusive ideas from popping up unexpectedly and I could direct my thinking down to the smallest detail.

The human mind is perhaps the single most powerful tool in all of nature. Human minds really did design and build battleships, after all. The tragedy is that most people never really tap into the full power of their mind. They let the weeds run roughshod over the garden. They serve their subconscious mind instead of making it serve them.

We all have heard stories about people who accomplish incredible, seemingly superhuman feats in times of extremity—the archetypal mother who finds the strength to lift a car off her child, for example, or the lost hiker who manages to survive for weeks without food or water. People perform surgery on themselves, cross deserts on foot, traverse entire oceans in homemade life rafts, and how do they do that? They use the power of their mind—specifically, their subconscious mind—to rewrite the story of what is happening to them, to highlight the hope and bury the pain, to visualize a positive outcome.

Even ordinary people who aren't trapped in life-or-death situations can use these techniques, however. In fact, honing your thinking in this way is the only consistent way that I've found to realize your purpose in this world.

This phase in The Way of the Quiet Warrior™ is all about building new mental muscles. Just like any other exercise program, it's going to be hard at first, and you may experience pain as you work through years of atrophy. Your reward, however, comes from seeing yourself grow in strength and efficacy. Soon, you will be able to accomplish things you'd never imagined you would!

A MEETING WITH
THE GODDESS

The sand and the sun were calling her name. At least, that's what Bert kept telling her. Allie was content, however, to stay inside, closed up tight in the dingy, Floridian bungalow they'd rented for the week. Inside had everything she needed: a pull-out sofa that dipped so low in the middle, her butt was practically touching the thin, hard carpeting; a fridge full of the finest rosé that seven dollars could buy; and a five-hundred-channel cable package that seemed to be airing at least one episode of *Judge Judy* at all times.

"You have to leave the house at some point," Bert told her, stinking of the sunscreen he caked on for his morning swims. It never seemed to work for him, though, and he was always somewhere in the midst of the white-guy-summer-skin cycle: burn, peel, burn again.

"To see what?" Allie asked him. "The endless blocks of condos? The liquor store on the corner?"

"The beach, Allison. The ocean. You know, the reason we came here?"

It wasn't, though. It wasn't the reason they had come at all. Canada has beaches and oceans too. It has vacation spots and getaways and cheap weekly rentals. They hadn't come to Florida for any of the things that were here, but for the things that weren't: the pitying looks, the earnest attempts at consolations, the half-finished nursery that hit her like a punch in the chest every time she walked by it.

It was true that none of those things were here in the bungalow, but that didn't mean they'd left *him* behind either. It never stopped surprising her how much he'd affected—was still affecting—their lives. Such a tiny little thing. A person they'd never even met, a person who never really *was,* and yet he had torn up everything in their life, like a bulldozer coming through and leaving just dead stumps and churned, exposed earth behind.

Here, at least, when Allie started thinking too much about *him,* though, she could close the curtains tighter and get some of that rosé out of the fridge, pop a Xanax or two, and be alone with the darkness, the dull murmuring of the television set. Back home, everyone wanted something from her, even if it was just a performance of grief. Here, no one cared about her. No one even knew she was here, except for Bert and he was busy burning himself up, swimming a thousand miles or whatever he did all day.

She knew that Bert was dealing with it in his own way, but that was sort of the problem. Bert was dealing with it. In a few weeks or months or years, he'd be ready to go back to the life they'd had before. With every day that passed, Allie doubted more and more that she'd ever be normal again. She couldn't tell him this. How would she even begin? "I think I'm broken. I think I'm gonna be broken forever?" And the not-telling sat in her belly like a sharp and bitter ulcer, paining her all the time.

Sometimes, he would try to hold her, and the feeling of it, his weight and his warmth and his arms around her made her feel like ants were crawling on her skin. He'd mostly quit trying now and Allison genuinely did not know if that was better or worse.

———————

"Did you check your e-mail today?" he asked over a dinner of soggy calamari from the seafood shack that Allie had never seen but knew existed because Bert picked up a meal there almost every day.

She nodded. She had not so much as opened her laptop since they'd arrived. Her phone battery had died on the flight and she hadn't bothered charging it.

"Any news from Chris?"

In the ever-expanding fiction that Allie was passively telling him, her former coworker Chris was on the lookout for her, sending her leads on consulting gigs. In reality, she hadn't spoken to Chris in six months.

"Nothing yet," she said.

Bert reached out and squeezed her knee. The constant exposure to the sun had managed to inject a little colour into him after all and their skin was almost the same shade now.

Absurdly, Allie thought of her mother, who wore a wide-brimmed sun hat and carried a parasol on top of that and how she had hated the way Allie would brown up in the summer. "You look like a field hand," she would chide in Kashmiri but in the summertime, nothing could keep Allie from the lake, the bike path, the soccer field; the whole world unfolded before her.

Her mother would think she was gorgeous right now, thinner and whiter than she'd ever been in her life.

"Something will turn up," Bert said, smiling at her and pushing over his Styrofoam container of fries.

Allie managed to smile back at him but the thought of actually eating anything made her stomach roll uncomfortably.

"I had a big lunch," she said and it was true, after a fashion. Two-thirds of a bottle of rosé certainly counted as overconsumption.

———————

When the doctor told them that the baby inside of her could not—would not—survive outside of the womb, Allie had an irrationally defiant thought: *we never wanted you anyway.* It felt, for a bizarre moment, as though the baby was rejecting the two of them, twisting himself into an unsurvivable knot rather than be born to Allie and Bert, and her first reaction, as usual, was to get her back up. He didn't want to be her son? Fine. She didn't *want* a child.

And she hadn't, at least, at first. It wasn't a planned pregnancy and she was almost thirty-eight when it happened, not exactly prime childbearing age. She had decided long ago—before she'd met Bert, even—that kids weren't in the cards for her. Her own parents were marginal at best and she'd never had that feeling that she'd heard other women describe, that deep, elemental drive to procreate.

She didn't hate kids either; she just . . . didn't think about them. Until she found out she was going to have one, that is. It had surprised her how excited Bert had been about the news. He was younger than she was and he'd never evinced any desire to have a child before, but, Allie realized, they'd never exactly talked about it either. His upbringing had been difficult in ways he'd never wanted to talk about and Allie had just assumed that he felt the same way she did. She started to wonder if she would be depriving him of something if she didn't have the baby.

The more she thought about it, the more she came around to the idea. She began to think that motherhood was something that she could do with the appropriate amount of help. Bert just got more and more enthusiastic and Allie thought that they'd do OK by the kid with one really good parent and one who was trying her best, and maybe a nanny or two.

The nanny was part of her early fantasy that she could have a baby without undue disruption of her career. She'd spent sixteen years, after all, building her reputation in the corporate world. She was known for thriving on crisis—for always being able to put in the longest hours, hop on the last-minute flights, take over the losing projects and turn them into winners. Surely her coworkers couldn't imagine that a child would derail her.

Yet, almost as soon as she began to show, she started feeling the push. At first, it was subtle: little jokes or comments about maternity leave and breast-feeding, but it eventually became real, pointed inquiries about how she intended to manage her time when the baby was born. She started hearing rumbles from the board every time she had to take off an hour or two for an appointment with her doctor, even though she was still performing at the highest levels.

She took an early maternity leave at five months, tired of proving herself to people she'd worked with for a decade, sick of justifying her time down to the minute like she was clocking in at a factory. It was as though the baby inside of her had transformed her into another person entirely, one deserving of mistrust and skepticism.

It was only supposed to be maternity leave, but Allie knew that, if she tried to come back, she would probably find herself pushed out in one fashion or another. She could figure out something after the baby was born, she had decided. Maybe she could start her own business and answer to no one but herself.

It was a plan, at least, until week twenty-two of her pregnancy, when everything collapsed.

"I didn't expect you to take it so hard," Allie's mother told her and Allie could practically hear the tight little frown in her voice. *Why are you still moping?* was what she meant. "I lost two pregnancies before you, you know," her mother added primly, like they were medals pinned to her chest.

But she hadn't lost Allie's child. *Hers.* Her son, who had changed the way she'd imagined her future and made her hopeful in a way she'd never felt before. Who had lived inside of her for five months, one week, and four days. Who had kicked when she played electronic music and demanded the spiciest Thai curry. It was her little baby who would never be.

Her mother was the most blunt about it, but she certainly wasn't the only person to express mild surprise at Allie's devastation. Everyone seemed to be thinking just what she had thought in the specialist's office that awful afternoon: that she'd never really wanted a child anyway, so what was the big deal?

The sentiment only got stronger the more time passed, and now, almost six months after they'd lost the baby, there was a little bit of baffled impatience behind the eyes of her friends and colleagues. Everyone in the world wanted Allie to just *be normal* again, and she would do it happily, if only she could.

Until then, she would take a pill to sleep and a pill to wake up and a pill to keep her mind slow and dull during the time in between. When pills failed, the rosé was close at hand.

———————

"Hey," Bert said, "I found something neat down by the shore."

"Like . . . a cool shell or something?" On the TV in front of her, a portly man was fidgeting under Judge Judy's wrathful stare.

"No, it's a place. You've gotta come see it."

Before Allie could even get out a demurral, Bert continued.

"It's our last night here," he said, "come out with me, please. I promise it won't take long."

She realized that this must be about the worst vacation imaginable for him. It had been the worst *everything* imaginable for him lately.

Allie levered herself off the sofa with difficulty.

"OK," she said, "but it better not be another hole-in-the-wall seafood place. I'm not getting food poisoning the night before we fly back."

———————

The walk felt strange. It was partially the novelty of moving around again after so long of lying in one place as motionless as possible, but it was mostly the feeling she'd had, ever since the termination, in fact, that her body was somehow transformed. She had changed over the course of the pregnancy and that felt natural and right, and Allie had felt sure she knew what to expect in the future.

It turned out, though, that she hadn't known. And then there was no baby and there was nothing inside her and she wasn't what she had been before and she wasn't what she had expected to become. Instead, there was an awful third option that she had never considered and she was still reckoning with the strangeness of it.

It was nearly sunset by the time they left the bungalow and Bert led her along an uneven blacktop path that paralleled the ocean. Allie could hear the waves but she couldn't quite see them in the gathering dark.

Their destination was highly visible, however, illuminated by moving neon lights that read *PALM READER* and blinked in and out periodically. Below that was an outward-facing palm, lines of bright neon moving across it in oblique patterns.

"Seriously?" Allie snorted. "I 'had to' see a fortune-teller?"

Bert held his hands up in front of him helplessly.

"Everyone I talked to here said if there is one thing in town you have to do, it's this. She's supposed to be really good."

"No one is good at telling the future," Allie said, thinking of her mother, who had long ago abandoned most of the religious and cultural practices of her childhood but still left food out for gods she no longer worshiped on Navreh—the new year. Allie had asked her why once and her mother had shrugged.

"It's important," she'd said, though Allie had the sense that she could not explain why. Maybe it was good, once in a while, to make space for the things that felt true.

"Fine," Allie said, "but you're paying." As souvenirs went, there were worse things to buy.

The woman—the fortune-teller—was probably in her forties or fifties and had a bustling, maternal energy, like she should be making pizza rolls for a group of preteens or something.

"Hi, honey," she said when Allie and Bert stepped in.

"Hi," Allie said, feeling weirdly shy. It occurred to her that she hadn't spoken to anyone except Bert since she'd arrived in Florida. Allie drifted around the interior of the little house, looking at the crystals and customized tarot sets on display. The woman seemed to see through her aimless wandering.

"You looking for a reading?" she asked and Allie managed to nod. "OK," the woman continued, "I do palms and I do these wooden-block things and, of course, I do the tarot. I have the Major Arcana for life's big questions and the Minor Arcana for everyday concerns."

It sounded a little bit like an infomercial but, almost immediately, Allie said, "Major Arcana, please." The woman smiled at her and tilted her head at the seat opposite her.

Bert hung back while Allie made herself comfortable. It was easy; there was a plush, embroidered pillow on the seat. The whole thing had a grandma's-house-meets-hippie-commune vibe.

"Cut the deck." The woman offered her a thin stack of cards that were twice as tall as an ordinary deck of cards and a little bit wider.

Allie cut the cards obediently and handed them back to the woman, who promptly began laying them out on the table in a pattern that seemed random to Allie but appeared to have great significance for the woman.

The woman chewed her lips and made contemplative noises in the back of her throat as she laid down the cards.

"I'm seeing water," she pronounced. It wasn't a promising start. Her house was less than a block from the beach; if Allie stood up now and looked out the right window, she could see water too.

"No," the woman mused, though Allie had not said anything. "Fresh water. Cold and deep and dark. I associate it with glaciers. Does that make sense?"

Allie shook her head dumbly.

"Water can sometimes mean rebirth, but I don't think so in this case . . . more like a transition or a transformation. But not *your* transformation." She tapped a long, unpolished fingernail on one card in particular. On it was a bizarre figure that appeared to be standing on one foot with the other bent over his thigh. There was a thick tree trunk right behind him. "This is the Hanged Man," the woman told her. "He's all about transformation, change, adaptability, but yours is inverted, see?" She briefly flipped the card so Allie could see how the card was supposed to look: the man upside down in a kind of suspended Spider-Man pose.

"There's a lot of inversion in your cards. Your Empress is upside down too. Fertility problems?" she peered at Allie's face. "No. Not that. You lost something, didn't you? A miscarriage?"

"N-not exactly," Allie managed, her voice strangled.

"Well, loss is all over these cards. But you've also got The Chariot and The Star in the upright position. That signifies triumph over adversity and positive influence over others. Like . . . a shepherd, I suppose you might say."

Allie wondered how she was supposed to shepherd anyone from her sofa, day-drinking until she passed out. It was the sort of idea she might have been attracted to once, back when she'd thought she might start her own business. But she had been a different person then.

"This is the big one, though," the woman warned. "You've gotta watch out for this upside-down moon. That's illusion, deception, and desperation. A lie you're being told. Or one you are telling yourself. That's what will cripple you, if you're not careful."

"Did you tell her?" Allie asked as they clambered over a low chain blocking cars from driving out onto the beach. Her feet slid uncomfortably in the loose sand. "About Little Bert?"

She saw him flinch a little when she said the name. They'd only decided on a name a few weeks before the termination. Allie wondered if this was the first time either of them had said it aloud since then.

He took her hand, leading her over a little pile of sea-slick rocks.

"No, I didn't tell her. Maybe you were sending out a vibe." He gave her a wan little smile. "Maybe she has magical powers."

"The people around here must think so, if they sent you her way. That, or they get a kickback from every reading." It felt good to joke with him. For weeks, their only communication had been strained updates about their day—or, in Allie's case, a lack of updates.

It was also the longest she'd gone without dosing herself with something, and that floating, detached feeling was starting to fade. She could feel the cold.

The tide was low and the beach extended out into a shapeless darkness. Only the sound of the waves hinted at the hugeness of what was in front of them.

"I think people probably see what they need to see in the cards." Bert crouched, clearing a place in the sand for Allie to sit down. Mercifully, the sand had held on to some of the day's heat and it was warm underneath her. The chill came off the water along with the overpowering odor of salt. "It's like how Ouija boards work."

"I thought Ouija boards *don't* work?" Allie took his hand again and pulled him down next to her.

"Well, I mean, you aren't talking to ghosts. But the little plastic thing—"

"Planchette."

"Yeah, the planchette. Anyway, that thing really *is* moving. It's just that the people playing are moving it. Not deliberately, not even consciously sometimes. I guess there are movements that are so small and so involuntary that we don't even realize we're making them."

They sat in silence for a moment after that, Allie digging a trench in the sand next to her.

"The brain is weird," Bert offered, his voice barely audible over the crashing of the waves. "It can do all sorts of things."

Allie thought about transformation and water and the stories that people told themselves, stories so powerful they could move a person's body. Stories that could keep people locked up inside their own heads.

Or stories that could open a door.

"What would you think," Allie said softly, "if I told you I didn't want to go back to corporate work? What if I wanted to build something of my own instead?"

Bert smiled at her. The skin on his nose had begun to peel. *He would have been a good dad,* Allie thought. But it wouldn't do to dwell on all the lives they didn't have.

"I would think that you could make that happen. I've always thought that about you."

"That I can make things happen?"

"That you can make *anything* happen."

4

PHASE FOUR

THE
BLUEPRINT

What are the specifics of your strategy?
What are the goals that create results?

So you've dug down deep inside, found that passion—that purpose—that can drive you forward to a real, successful vision for your future. You are primed and ready, electrified by your new purpose and eager to make all your dreams into realities.

But how do you do that? The same way we accomplish anything of real value and ambition: with a plan.

In many respects, our DMP is just like any other BHAG (Big, Hairy, Audacious Goal); it is best accomplished by breaking it down into smaller and smaller steps, eating the elephant one bite at a time, as the old saying goes. We also need to be flexible and willing to incorporate new knowledge as we move further and further along in our journey. As an example, here is my written vision as it existed in October of 2012 (my top two needs linked to this DMP were Legacy and Autonomy):

I am elated and filled with emotion, having finished my book on or before September 17, 2015. I have become a beacon of light for children and young adults growing up with addicted parents. I began my journey traveling and speaking to one child or one person at a time, collecting stories and sharing my own experience. I have put these stories out into the world where they can provide a point of connection for others and even save lives. These children and their families are my legacy.

I have been working for years toward my goal of transforming an industry, toward creating wealth for the many versus the few, and that dream is coming true on or before September 2014. Having been a corporate-change agent in the past, creating enormous wealth for the already wealthy and privileged, it has been a blessing to partner up with industry legends and implement the Qivana Success System.

I have mastered this system and become a top achiever in Qivana. I collaborated with the company in a meeting of the minds, which produced a best-selling book and created interest among leaders both here and abroad.

My schedule is packed, booked solid for the next year at speaking engagements in which I discuss how I transformed an industry. After years of being a change agent in several industries, I have found freedom in my ability to show ordinary people around the world the power of change and transformation.

When I woke up this morning, I felt fortunate. My financial legacy for my children is nearly complete. I've achieved this on or before September 17, 2015. We are heading to the UK soon to visit my daughter as she nears earning her master's degree at Oxford University. Our boys are back home, settled into houses that we helped them purchase. The trust funds we set up for our children ensure that they will be looked after for the rest of their lives.

After our UK trip, we are planning an expedition to Italy, where I will take cooking courses. On or before September 2016, I will open a restaurant in Canada. It will be a gathering place for families, friends, and communities, incorporating elements from all the many cultural elements of our family. It will be a safe place where people feel comfortable relaxing and creating positive memories with their loved ones.

Eventually, Anna and I will retreat to our summer home overlooking Osoyoos Lake in the Okanagan region, where we'll relax and recharge before embarking upon a world tour. It is incredibly freeing to have no constraints on our time or our finances.

I am nearing the completion of a foundation I've worked to establish with a group of my fellow millionaires. We will finalize the legal papers on this initiative on or before September 2016 and invest at least a million dollars, collectively, into the fund, which is designed to fuel initiatives that further the survival of mankind and the planet in general. We are interested in initiatives to build schools and wells in developing countries, to create resources funds, boost infrastructure, and assist disadvantaged youth across the globe.

I have found it easy—and satisfying—to give up or trade things to accomplish these goals. I no longer miss TV during the week, nor do I spend time and mental energy on morbid crime dramas. Choosing not to reenter the workforce as a hired executive feels incredible, and I've transcended my old behavioral models built on fear, failure, and rejection—and it is amazing.

I have stripped down my life, removing the frivolous luxuries that can so easily become necessities if we allow that to happen. Giving beyond myself and helping others is incredibly nourishing. In October 2009, it became clear what parts of my life I would need to jettison to complete my own Hero's Journey, and I am constantly working on that journey, writing and rewriting my future as I go. I use the power of my subconscious mind to break old paradigms and establish new, positive behaviors. My purpose drives and supports me, spurring me on to success.

Ambitious enough for you? A lot of people would tell you—and did tell me—that my vision was crazy, that those things would never happen. It was true that almost everything in my vision was a statistical long shot, but that is the nature of a true purpose. If no one ever set out to do unlikely or even impossible things, we would have no innovations, no records, no growth, and no exploration. The fastest runner in the world is always unbeatable until someone beats him or her. The next step in technology is always science fiction until someone makes it reality. All of human history is the story of people pushing the boundaries of what is possible.

That is not to say, however, that my vision was fixed and immutable, unchanged from the moment I put it down on paper. As I noted in the last segment of my vision, I fully intended to change and adapt elements of the document as I learned more about myself and the path I was following. To see that change in action, I give you my most recent DMP from October 2016:

My Personal Pivotal Needs are legacy, true health, and happiness. I am elated and filled with emotion, having finished my book on or before September 17, 2017. I have become a beacon of light for children and young adults growing up with addicted parents. I began my journey traveling and speaking to one child or one person at a time, collecting stories and sharing my own experience. I have put these stories out into the world, where they can provide a point of connection for others and even save lives. These children and their families are my legacy.

Having implemented my new company, I've changed an industry and my income is consistently $30,000 a month as of September 2019. I begin work on my second book, taking thirty years of experience as "Tommy Gun, corporate fixer" and drawing a parallel between my career as a change agent in the corporate world to my work in creating change in the lives of individuals and families. This is an awesome shift in my purpose and I feel as though I am truly living the dream.

My financial legacy for my children is complete on or before September 2019, and Anna and I have ensured a solid financial future for all of our children. Our daughter is working on her fourth year of university, and whenever I look at her and her rich, satisfying life, I am delirious with joy. Financial wealth gives Anna and I the freedom to be with our daughter, our boys, and our grandchild at any time and place, and offer them incredible experiences.

Physically, I am in peak condition, feeling like a thirty-year-old, with boundless energy and true health. We are leaving for Italy soon, where I will take cooking courses and my wife Anna will guide us through a tour she has devised of her birthplace in Rome. I am elated because my dream of becoming a world-class chef is coming true. After I complete my schooling, my new restaurant will open in Vancouver on or before September 2017. It will be a blend of Indian and Italian cultures and culinary traditions, and it will function as a peaceful gathering place for friends and family.

On or before September 17, 2018, The Way of the Quiet Warrior™ Fund has been established with my business partner. We've developed a comprehensive list of causes we'd like to provide with donations annually. We are going to make the world a better, healthier, and greater place.

I am a Hero in my own life and my new blueprint is firing on all cylinders. I use the power of my subconscious mind to break old paradigms and establish new, positive behaviors. My purpose drives and supports me, spurring me on to success.

As you can see, many of the same elements are in place across both DMPs. I've sharpened some ideas, added details or smaller, incremental goals to them, and other things have changed entirely. A few things, like the focus on true health, are entirely new.

You will notice that I used very careful, idiosyncratic phrasing in both visions and that was by design. Once again, it's about harnessing the power of the subconscious mind. When I use particular words and phrases, that can trigger something in my subconscious mind to get it working toward—or focusing on—that idea. When my subconscious is working on an idea, that is the first step toward actually manifesting that idea.

I also make sure to include descriptions of how I feel as I accomplish these goals and that is critical. Oftentimes when we set goals, we imagine that we must be as dispassionate and straightforward as possible, but that is not how the DMP works. Your purpose is inextricably linked to your feelings and how you experience that purpose will make the difference between succeeding and failing.

We use similar visualization tactics to those in Phase Three here to learn how to project ourselves in the future and describe how it feels to be there, living that dream. Having that specific description is critical in terms of getting us from the present to that future. If you are not aware of your emotions, you can't use them to motivate yourself, and if you can't motivate yourself, you will not be able to complete your journey.

It is that element of motivation, more than anything else that sets The Way of the Quiet Warrior™ apart from any other similar practice. Making a sterile list of all the things you must accomplish or all the changes you need to make is all well and good, but we do not believe that anyone can make real progress unless he or she knows why those changes have to be made, why those particular things must be accomplished, and what purpose those things will actually serve. If you have a strong vision for the future linked to your deepest passions and infused with emotion, you can put all the steps of the plan in context and know exactly how everything you're doing today will help you create your chosen tomorrow.

When I was creating a written version of my DMP and looking honestly at the things I genuinely needed in my life, I developed my own personal PPNs (first Legacy and Autonomy, and then Legacy, True Health, and Happiness). With those in place, I started breaking those ideas into smaller goals.

My four big goals, intended to address all of my PPNs, were:

1. Achieve a weight of 165 lbs. on or before December 31, 2014. (True Health)
2. Achieve a residual income of $30,000 a month on or before December 31, 2015. (Autonomy)
3. Create a legacy fund for my family and children of $300,000 on or before December 31, 2016. (Legacy)
4. Open a restaurant and become a home chef on or before December 31, 2017. (Happiness)

The next steps probably won't be unfamiliar to anyone who has done any work in the corporate sector: I developed a blueprint that had specific goals, outlined steps to meet those goals, and provided a timeline for everything. I did this the same way I would have if I were starting a business or launching some new initiative. There are a number of very good, time-tested methods for developing a plan of action and I am glad to utilize them. It is really the work that we do in Phase One through Phase Three that makes this process unique.

Here, I would like to share an anecdote that I heard from a number of leaders, speakers, educators, and other professionals invested in motivating people to meet their goals. Yale University performed a study on goal setting, and they found that the participants who wrote their goals down were 80 percent more likely to achieve those goals than those who did not write anything down.

That's a powerful factoid, right? In the business world, that story would be called a "teaching tool," designed to show people the incredible power of concrete goal setting, and it's very effective.

The problem is, none of it is true.

A friend of mine, a very effective educator who does incredible speaking tours and he, of course, had encountered this anecdote about the Yale study from many of his contemporaries. Only my friend did something that almost no one else did: he actually checked on the veracity of the story. He and his business partner actually called Yale University to inquire about this study and perhaps get more details, and they were astonished to discover that the study had never taken place. It was a totally fictitious anecdote—basically, the business world's version of an urban legend. Just like stories of spiders in a beehive hairdo or hook-handed madmen attacking frisky teenagers, the Yale-study story was designed to illustrate a lesson, and it did that so successfully that it became ubiquitous.

In reality, we have no idea what writing down goals does in terms of increasing your chances of achieving those goals. In my personal experience, though, I would wonder if this sort of thinking could actually make a person less likely to meet his or her goals. If you believe that writing things down is taking a significant, concrete step toward achieving your dreams, you might be inclined to simply leave it at that: writing down the exact same goals with no change or progress for years on end.

I tend to believe that any program for success that is built upon a lie is going to fail. It all comes back to that idea of motivation. If you are doing things for the wrong reasons—reasons that aren't real or don't exist—you can't really understand and modify your behavior to get different outcomes.

I am not going to tell you that Yale or Harvard or even the local community college has studied The Way of the Quiet Warrior™ program, but I can tell you that these practices have worked for me, and I've seen them work for others as well.

The Way of the Quiet Warrior™ program doesn't just stop at writing down goals, though that is a great initial step. Once we have those goals, we break them down into steps and we put those steps into a clear timeline. Then we project our feelings and our mental state along that timeline so we can clearly envision what our life will be like as we move forward, meeting all of these smaller interim goals. We are creating a blueprint for our future, with all the component parts clearly labeled and ready to be assembled.

At the same time, we are also creating a kind of "thought blueprint" for ourselves. I learned in Phase Three that our modes of thinking are incredibly powerful and we want to make sure that we are thinking positively and constructively. We want our thoughts to benefit us, not hold us back. Creating a blueprint is as much about developing a certain kind of mind-set as it is about laying out a series of actions.

In my case, you could look at a goal like "$30,000 monthly income" and think that it is a totally pie-in-the-sky fantastical idea. I knew, however, from my own experience so far, that I could have that kind of monthly income because I had done it before. When I was embedded in the corporate world, we averaged about $30,000 per month. If I had done that in a job that was killing me on every level, why couldn't I do it when I was happy, healthy, and completely in control of my own career? Of course, if my goal were to do something that I'd never experienced before, I could still make that happen, but I would probably require the help of someone else who did have that experience—but that's something we'll get to in the last two phases.

I started with that knowledge that what I wanted to do was possible and then I began to analyze the goal, looking for ways to segment it into smaller goals. Remember, one bite at a time allows us to eat the elephant. First, I established my timeline. Some goals are things you want to happen immediately, but most are things that you want to project into the future. So I gave myself a number of years to get to that $30,000 figure. Then, I had to establish the mechanism by which I was going to meet this goal. Just like any other journey, you have to figure out what vehicles are best to get you where you're going. You wouldn't take an airplane from your house to the grocery store, just like you wouldn't ride a unicycle from Moscow to Paris.

In my case, the vehicle was something that I hadn't even considered. Back when I was originally making $30,000 per month, my vehicle was my position in the corporate world and my work as a CEO. When I was creating my blueprint, that was an option on the table. I could have gone back to my work as "Tommy Gun," helping ailing companies and serving as a temporary leader. I knew, however, that diving back into that world would actively set back many of my other goals, especially the goals I had in terms of my own personal development. I couldn't help but wish then that I'd discovered all this years before. Not only would I have been more effective as a leader, but I also would have had a certain economic safety net. TELUS's downsizing of my division of the company left me at a fork in the road, career-wise, but that's not necessarily true for everyone. Many people are able to move through all six phases while remaining in the same career and even the same job. It all comes down to your DMP and whether or not your career is furthering that.

In my case, it wasn't really doing so, so I nixed the idea of chasing down my old career, which left me with no choice but to try something new. I found the idea of being my own boss very compelling but I wasn't sure exactly how to go about doing that. How do I launch my own company? How can I cover my living expenses while getting something like that off the ground? How could I ensure that this was something that would yield long-term success?

It was during this time that, with Anna's permission, I became something of a seeker. Instead of doing what I'd done my entire life—what I was "supposed" to do—I allowed myself to follow my instincts. When I felt drawn to a person or a company or an event, I went and tried to be as open as possible to the experience.

This led me to creating all sorts of connections with people from just about every walk of life and all the industries you can imagine, from government to health care to infrastructure. After one Tony Robbins event called "Wealth Mastery" (I had gone there searching for ways to build wealth), I got a fateful call from a young woman who had just happened to have been in the audience with me. She wanted to know if I was interested in getting into network marketing.

The company—Qivana—dealt in natural health products, and that was something that had become very important to me during my health journey. I had never worked for a network marketing company before, and it is true that some of these companies don't have the best reputation, but I was willing to take a closer look at how the business worked.

The company was created by CEO Derek Hall, former president of Nature's Way, one of the largest natural health brands in the nation. He is also the former CSO of McKesson, the largest drug company in the world. I liked Derek and I liked the product line. I personally credited natural health solutions with helping me recover from years of a toxic go-go-go lifestyle. So I decided to give Qivana a shot.

Just as I had done in the corporate world, I very quickly advanced in network marketing. In just a year and a half, I became a diamond distributor, which is one of the highest sales tiers in the company. I was bringing in significant money and making strides toward my monthly income goal. What I discovered, however, was that I was getting the most satisfaction out of helping others to be successful in the industry.

One thing I like about network marketing is the low barrier to entry. You don't need an advanced degree or years of experience; you don't even need to leave your house if that's what you choose. It rewards work ethic and allows people to launch their own businesses, and I was discovering that many of my fellow marketers were a lot like me: people who had suffered and lost everything and who were in the process of building themselves back up. I really enjoyed getting to meet with them and hear their stories, and I started building teams of distributors around the world, something that benefited everyone involved.

Network marketing was clearly part of the solution to my financial problem and personal health plan, but it wasn't enough on its own. Recall that at that time, I wasn't just trying to get my monthly income back on track; I was also attempting to dig our family out of the deficit caused by the huge losses we had suffered. I resigned myself to the idea that I couldn't completely get out of the corporate world, but I tried to position myself as more of a consultant than a leader. If I was going to be in the corporate world, I at least wanted to be in an advisory position rather than striving, as I had before, simply to make money for distant shareholders.

I found that, in many ways, my new vocations dovetailed. I had never realized before how many high-level executives were struggling with many of the same problems I'd experienced. I saw men and women who were desperately unhappy and unable to admit that to themselves. Many of them had the same health problems that I'd had; they were overweight and overmedicated, eating poor-quality food and never finding the time to exercise. Many of them were dependent upon substances—especially alcohol—to simply power through their stressful and unhappy lives. I saw many careers ended by heart attacks, strokes, advanced diseases, all things that could be directly related to the poor health of these top-level leaders.

I felt sure that I had something to offer to these people, and something was slowly starting to percolate in my head. I began to feel that the corporate world—corporate life, at least—was a component part of my larger purpose and I just had to find the correct way to fit it in.

That really was a challenge because all of the negative parts of some corporate cultures were definitely still lurking. Even in my new role, I found myself bumping up against all the things that had originally kept me from returning in the first place. I lost jobs because of the new boundaries I was willing to draw. I gave up clients because they'd asked me to choose between network marketing and working for their firm. Trusting my gut very often meant walking away from money, sometimes significant amounts of money.

As those situations began to pile up, I began to feel torn. Corporate work gave me money and stability, and there was something there that I found compelling. I knew the kinds of personalities that gravitated toward leadership positions, and I had increasingly come to feel that I was uniquely equipped to help them become happier and more effective. At the same time, I was wary of committing to any one position, especially when it required me to close off other avenues. I wasn't sure if network marketing was something I wanted to do in the long term, but I knew I did want to explore it more and I didn't want to give up my freedom pursue other career pathways. To return to the metaphor of the jigsaw puzzle, I had the box with the picture of what I was working toward, and I was collecting more puzzle pieces all the time, but I hadn't quite figured out how they fit together.

It was actually one of those moments of incongruity that led me to a huge breakthrough. I was working with a leader who I'd identified as toxic and I was trying to course-correct with him. He had actually become connected with Jon LoDuca of The Wisdom Link in Holland, Michigan, but some aspect of Jon's work had displeased him. So, while I was in the room, this leader called Jon up and just went off on him. It was a brutal dressing-down; he was tearing into Jon in a way that I knew from having worked closely with him for weeks, was unfair. As I saw it, the leader could not cope with Jon's autonomy and boundary setting. The leader needed to feel that he could control everyone he worked with and Jon had resisted that idea.

I was incredibly uncomfortable during this entire call, embarrassed by the unprofessional way that leader was handling this issue and feeling torn by my sense that Jon was not in the wrong. After that happened, I found that I couldn't stop thinking about it and I even did a little bit of research about Jon and his company. The more I read, the more intrigued I became; it turned out, Jon had a specific program, called "Innovation Lab™," for people who wanted to create their own businesses, and I couldn't get that idea out of my head. I knew that creating a business was an option to realizing my DMP, but, up until that point, I hadn't been exactly sure where to start.

It cost $7,500 to attend the program; plus, I would need to fly to Michigan. All to meet with someone whom I had never formally met, to complete a course that was new and unfamiliar. Still, it wouldn't let me go. I talked it over with Anna, who agreed with me that I needed to go with my Blue-personality instincts. If this was how I was going to live my life, it needed to start right away.

So I went to Michigan and it was there that Jon helped me pull together all the disparate pieces of the puzzle. What we developed there combined all the things I'd learned about corporate life, the joy I got from helping people, the importance of connection and sharing my story, the specific experience I had, and the expertise I'd developed. What we came away with was the first, tentative form of The Way of the Quiet Warrior™.

Over the next year, Jon was my guide. He helped build the brand, the business process and assets, and supported my efforts along the way.

As I worked toward my specific goal of hitting a certain monthly income, I had moved forward step by step, but I had also allowed each one of those steps to teach me things and to inform many other aspects of my life. Not only did breaking the goal into smaller goals help me succeed, but it also actually allowed me to gain perspective on my larger purpose beyond the simple numbers game of a monthly income. Without a blueprint that included and encompassed all of my goals, personal and professional, I would not have been able to create this business that is perfectly in line with my own values. Because I came to Jon with my DMP already in place, I was also able to do something a little unconventional. I developed a business that was not actually focused around me, personally, but one that would create a place where I could help people directly and make income in an ongoing way. That income, in turn, would allow me to devote time and energy to other elements of my DMP.

All the tools were in place. I had a specific vision of the future that I was moving toward. It was linked to the most important parts of myself, the needs and motivations that drove me, and now I had a blueprint—a plan with goals, action steps, and timelines. Now, I had to actually build up the courage to launch that plan into being. I had to take that first enormous step on an uncertain journey.

I had no idea what was going to happen when I started on that pathway, but I knew one thing for certain: I could not do it alone.

INDELIBLE

The blonde girl was definitely drunk. She had that unmistakable glaze in her eyes and whenever Stephen asked her a question, she just gave him a big, slow grin and didn't answer. Her friend (the redhead) was probably a little tipsy herself, but was handling it much better. Red did the talking.

"We want portraits. Of each other. But, like, as those sexy '40s girls, you know?" She patted her right shoulder. "We want them here. About this big," she added, spreading out her fingers as wide as they would go. Even if Stephen worked on drunk people (which he didn't), there was no way he was doing a giant back piece on anyone who couldn't pass a Breathalyzer test.

He couldn't say that directly to her, however. There were few creatures that contained more undiluted belligerence than drunk undergrads, and they resented nothing more than being reminded that they were, in fact, drunk undergrads.

"You're talking about a pretty big piece," Stephen began cautiously, and the redhead gave him a satisfied nod. "You know that's more than one session, right?"

"Sure," Red seemed blithe and unconcerned, but her blonde companion knit up her face in a childlike pout. Which made sense, Stephen supposed, because this time last year, Blondie was probably nagging her mom to give her a lift to lacrosse practice.

"Naaaah," the blonde drawled. "Do it in one. We're tough."

"It's not about toughness." Stephen had heard the same objections from beefy gym rats and multi-pierced goth girls, and they were all wrong. "It's not great for me, working on someone for hours at a time. You want the best possible art? Break up the job into sessions. It's like building a house; you do a blueprint and take it one step at a time."

"How bad can it hurt?" Blondie interrupted, apparently having absorbed nothing of what Stephen had said. "I broke both my arms in primary school *and* I had to get knee surgery." She raised one leg into the air awkwardly, like a cheerleader with a head injury.

"It feels like being stung by a wasp, but over and over again in the same place," the redhead said, her voice much quieter now. She was mulling over Stephen's advice; he could see it on her face. Maybe if he could convince her that tonight wasn't the night for her grand experiment in body art, the both of them would leave without incident and Stephen could go back to his viable customers.

The blonde cocked her head curiously.

"My mom told me," Red offered quietly. There must have been something up with Redhead's mom because Blondie got that look on her face like people do when a sad subject comes up and they don't know what to say.

"Your mom has ink?" Stephen asked

"Sort of," Redhead was uncomfortable. This clearly wasn't something she liked to discuss.

"You should talk it over with her. See what she says, she might have some advice for you. Sleep on it, figure out what you want, then come back here and I'll fix you up."

Blondie was still annoyed, but the mention of Red's mother had thrown a wet blanket over the room and Blondie didn't look like she wanted to pick a fight anymore.

"All right." Red smiled and took her friend's hand. "Let's go get tacos!"

Blondie brightened and Stephen could practically see all thoughts of tattoos fleeing her mind.

"Tacos!" she enthused.

———————

Stephen didn't expect to see either of them ever again, so he was a little confused on Monday afternoon when Jean, at the front desk, told him that "a little chick" wanted to see him. Red looked more pulled together, older, in the full light of day. She had a scrubbed, makeup-free face and a manila folder in her hand, like she was going to the principal's office.

"Hey," she said when Stephen came around the register. "That offer to fix me up still good?"

"You eighteen?"

Red nodded.

"You sober?"

"Yup."

"Then, it's still good; come on back."

"I still want a retro style," Red launched into an eager explanation as soon as they got back to the tattoo room. "But now I'm thinking more Rosie the Riveter than Betty Page."

"And what about your girl? What does she want?"

Red grimaced.

"Caitlin actually already got her tattoo."

"In two days?"

"She got it . . . that same night, actually. She couldn't wait anymore, even after we'd had tacos."

She must have gone to one of those shady scratchers on Wind Street. They were undoubtedly used to inking teenagers with a taco in one hand and a shot in the other.

"What'd she get?"

"It's kind of a bird," Red answered diplomatically.

"Kind of?"

Red lowered her voice. "I think it looks more like a flying IUD. But she seems happy."

Funny how that had happened, Stephen thought. *This bird piece doesn't sound anything like what Blondie had described to me but, nevertheless, she now considers the whole experience a triumph. It isn't uncommon; some people just want to get tattooed and they don't really care much about the design.*

Red clearly did, though, and she'd brought Stephen a bunch of photos and printouts of images that she liked.

"I'd like you to get as close to this as possible for the face," she said, passing him a glossy photograph stubbled with pinpricks in all the corners. It was probably ten years old and it featured a freckly kid that Stephen took to be Red as a child. She was wrapped up in the arms of a young woman with the same wavy, crimson hair and the same long, blunt nose that you might see on Greek pottery.

"Your mom?" Stephen asked and Red nodded.

Stephen pushed her a little bit on the size of the tattoo and the complexity, but Red never backed down.

"It takes as long as it takes," she said when he warned her that he would want to string the sessions out over a few weeks. Then she hung over Stephen's shoulder as he sketched, offering suggestions and corrections until they had a design that they agreed upon: a large, three-quarter-view portrait of a woman wearing a kerchief and a retro jumpsuit. She had a wry but determined expression and Red's same bright hair peeking out from her kerchief.

"Perfect," Red said, grinning.

———

The first sitting was the longest. Stephen liked to do it that way so he could get as much work done as possible while the customer was still fresh. He also liked to use that first session to get a gauge for how much the person could take. Some people couldn't manage at all; they were twitching and squirming as soon as he touched the needle to their skin. Most people lasted longer but everyone came to a point where his or her endurance failed and then began to shift underneath his tattoo gun.

Red had a high tolerance; she sat rock-still for the first forty-five minutes. Stephen could tell that it was taking all her energy not to move, though, because she made it clear that she didn't want to talk, giving his questions curt yes-or-no answers.

"You and your mom are close?" he asked when he gave her a break to get some water and stretch.

"Yup. It was always just the two of us, so we kinda had to be close." On her shoulder, an image of the woman was starting to take place, a hard, thick outline of her face and shoulder.

Stephen gestured toward his own right bicep on which he had a fierce Japanese-style mermaid coiled in a fighting posture.

"I always think of this one as being for my mom. When she was young, she used to spend her summers working at this resort down in Florida. They had this big aquarium that people could walk through, with all these colourful fish, and then girls like my mom would dress up in mermaid outfits, the tail and all, and they'd swim around in there. She said the kids loved it."

Red smiled at him, kind of shyly.

"That's really cool. Did she teach you how to swim?"

Stephen laughed.

"Nah. She held out until I was about ten, but she wasn't really cut out for motherhood, you know? She dumped me on my grandparents and then went off to do . . . whatever she wanted to do. She was kind of a wild thing."

"Like a mermaid," Red offered, clambering back onto the chair.

"Yeah," Stephen smiled. "Like a mermaid."

———

In the second session, Stephen finished the outline and started the fill: the brilliant red of her hair and the dull powder blue of her jumpsuit—tiny, dark freckles across her minuscule face.

"Did it make you feel better?" This session seemed to be a little easier on Red now that she knew what to expect. She could talk this time, at least. "Getting your mermaid tattoo?"

"Better about my mom, you mean?" Stephen asked and Red almost moved her head to nod before she caught herself and simply said, "Yes."

"Sort of." Stephen hadn't really thought about it, but, upon reflection, it had felt a little bit like a purging. Or an exorcism. The pain of it and the image that remained afterward was a permanent, external reminder of something that was never really very far from his mind.

"I think it can be a kind of therapy," Stephen offered. "Or part of therapy, at least. Marking yourself . . . it feels important."

Red knew better now than to move but Stephen could tell that, if she could have, she would have nodded.

The colour was the toughest part. He had to strike a balance between clarity and strength, find something that wouldn't fade after a year or two, but which didn't overpower the delicate shape of the face. One blurred line, one missed curve and poor Red would wind up with a wonky-looking Rosie permanently tattooed on her shoulder.

"So, have you told your mom you're getting this?"

"I figured I'd surprise her," Red answered.

"Yeah, parents typically love that."

"She will. I know her." Red fell silent and he thought she wasn't going to say anything else, but then she added in the softest voice, "I know her better than anyone."

"Well, you said she had some ink herself, so she can't get too mad."

Red stiffened slightly, like she was holding in a breath or a word.

"You know about radiation?"

"Like Chernobyl?"

"Like for getting rid of cancer."

"Not too much," Stephen said evenly.

"Well, I do." Red suddenly sounded so much older than just eighteen. "When they give you radiation, they don't just do it once and they don't do it all over. They have to target it, put a target on you, basically. They draw it on you, sometimes with permanent marker, but if you don't want to bother with being careful about showering, getting it redone, all that, or if you—" her voice cracked slightly but she recovered almost immediately, "if you are gonna have a lot of radiation, you can get the marks tattooed on your body."

"Where are your mom's marks?"

"On her chest. Where her breasts were."

Some people said that the colour filling was the worst part of the process; the needle just went over and over the same battered patch of skin, deeply pushing in the ink. Red didn't seem bothered, though, not nearly so much as the first time. If she was hurting, it wasn't from Stephen's gun.

"You're not from here, are you?" Red asked Stephen.

"Nope. From the good ol' US of A. Georgia, specifically."

"Yeah, you've got a bit of an accent."

Stephen smiled.

"Well, as far as I'm concerned, it's you who talks funny."

She almost laughed at that but stilled herself so as not to disrupt the needle. They were almost done now and Stephen had saved the thinnest, most precise lines of the face for last.

"What brought you all the way to BC?"

It was a good question, one that Stephen had asked himself repeatedly during his first few months in the city, when he was still adapting to the shock of winter and the dearth of familiar faces.

"This is the only thing I've ever wanted. A tattoo parlor, I mean. My grandparents both died a few years back and they left me everything they had. Not a fortune or anything but enough to get something started. Doing anything other than the thing I'd wanted most seemed almost like wasting it, you know?"

"This is a good place," Red agreed. "I'm glad you opened it."

"Well, thanks. I try to do professional work."

"It's not just the work. It's . . . I dunno. It's the way you do it, it's . . . helpful."

"I always strive to be helpful," Stephen said drily.

———————

When the tat was finally finished, Stephen gave her a hand mirror and let her check it out in the big wall mirrors that ringed the room. Before she went home, he'd cover the piece with gauze and give her all her cleaning supplies so it would heal properly, but for now, he'd give her a minute to admire her new artwork.

"I love it," Red beamed, still struggling to look over her shoulder even though she had the hand mirror. "It's perfect; you really got her. That's her face. That's my mom's face." For a moment, Stephen wondered if she was going to cry. This tattoo parlor was no stranger to emotional outbursts, but usually not quite for this reason.

"Thank you," she said, turning to look at him. "It's so much better than flying birth control."

"That's a low bar to clear, but I'll take it."

"I feel . . . different," Red enthused, rolling her shoulder. "Like I put on some armor or something. Is it always like that?"

Stephen thought about how he'd felt when his mermaid piece was completed. He hadn't felt armored; instead, he'd felt lighter, unburdened. Some old hurt inside him had eased a little bit.

"I don't think it's the same for everyone, but I think, for the right person at the right moment, the right ink can be just what you need to get through something. Or move on from something."

Red smiled at him, her eyes shining.

"Hey," he said, "if I don't see you again, I want to tell you good luck. With your mom."

Red shrugged.

"Cancer's like a lot of things. You make your plan and you carry it out a little bit at a time. And when you're done . . ." she trailed off, gesturing toward the image of her mother, eternally young, eternally determined, always at her shoulder.

"When you're done," Stephen said softly, "you're not the same person anymore."

5

THE
LAUNCH

How will you get in motion?
Who will walk with you?

The Cat only grinned when it saw Alice. It looked good-natured, she thought; still it had VERY long claws and a great many teeth, so she felt that it ought to be treated with respect.

"Cheshire Puss,'" she began, rather timidly, as she did not at all know whether it would like the name; however, it only grinned a little wider. "Come, it's pleased so far," thought Alice, and she went on. "Would you tell me, please, which way I ought to go from here?"

"That depends a good deal on where you want to get to," said the Cat.

"I don't much care where—" said Alice.

"Then it doesn't matter which way you go," said the Cat.

T he above is a selection from Lewis Carroll's *Alice in Wonderland* and it has a surprising amount of relevance for many people struggling to manifest their purpose. By the time we reach the fifth phase in The Way of the Quiet Warrior™, we have one advantage over Alice: our blueprint linked to our DMP and backed by that burning desire we have discovered tells us exactly where we *want* to go. Getting there, however, still requires the assistance of an experienced guide (though ideally, one less cryptic than the Cheshire Cat!).

Phase Five is called THE LAUNCH because it is the portion of the unique process in which we actually help propel the client toward his or her goals, and a critical part of that is the use of a guide. I've been intrigued by the role and function of mentor figures ever since I looked more deeply into Campbell's Hero's Journey arc. He posits that part of every Hero's Journey is the moment when, after returning from an arduous and transformative trip, the Hero has the option to return to the "known" world and provide guidance for others who may benefit from his or her experience.

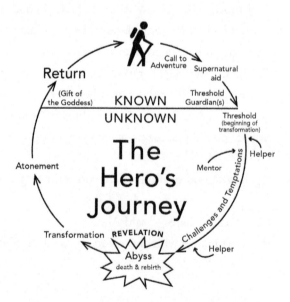

I quickly realized that I, personally, was very drawn to the role of "guide," and when I was developing The Way of the Quiet Warrior™, I knew that I had to include a strong element of mentorship. In my experience, those times when I tried to succeed without the help of a guide were some of the most difficult and dispiriting parts of my life and career. When I did connect with a knowledgeable and empathetic guide, I found that I made greater and greater strides toward all of my goals.

No matter how strong your sense of purpose is or how rock-solid your conviction, it is easy to get lost and fall off the path if you are doing it all alone. Some personalities have a strong preference—even a compulsion—to work alone, but we all have to compromise occasionally. You need someone by your side with a compass, a map, and a good head on his or her shoulders. This may seem like a commonsense idea but it can actually be quite difficult to get people to really understand how helpful a mentor can be.

Working, as I do, with people who are professionals used to being successful and being in leadership positions can be exhilarating and fun but it can also be difficult. These are hard-charging people—many of them, Red personalities—who are used to doing things on their own and they often believe that not only do they not need help to meet their goals, but also that outside assistance will actually slow them down or inhibit their ability to formulate new ideas. I do know that many leaders value feedback from advisory boards or boards of directors. What I am speaking of here is a more personal one-on-one relationship.

When I was a CEO, I didn't truly understand my limitations until my first 360-degree survey, which shocked me with the results I got. Unfortunately, the higher you climb in a company, the more removed you are from the reality of everyone around you. You are in a bubble of sorts and some people get very comfortable in that bubble. They actively avoid the opinions of outsiders out of fear of hearing something negative—of someone taking a pin to the bubble.

In my experience, the people who most devalue the utility of a mentor or a guide are people who have never had really good guidance. Once you've had the experience of having a smart person in your corner, who has gone through his or her own Hero's Journey and is eager to help you, trying to do it solo feels pointlessly difficult.

I know how these fiercely independent leaders feel, though, because I was in their same position not so long ago. When I was working as an hired-gun CEO and trying to turn companies around, I felt an enormous pressure—both internal and external—to handle everything myself. "It's lonely at the top" has become a cliché for a reason: there's more than a bit of truth in it. A CEO doesn't really have a "boss" as such, but he or she is accountable to a large and diffuse group of people, including shareholders, board members, and company employees. There is no one person, however, with whom a leader can easily talk through problems and frustrations. I, myself, ruined many family dinners with my wife by venting endlessly about the office.

In my case, I was actually provided with a coach who had a background in psychology, and she was able to use those skills to really tailor her advice to me and my specific needs. Unfortunately, her job was really only to help me integrate into the company at the beginning of my tenure as CEO, and, after three months, her role was phased out. I had really valued my time with her. She had pointed out a lot of blind spots and ways of thinking that were holding me back and we had worked together to break through those roadblocks. I hadn't felt like our work was completed when she left. She had shown me a lot about what I was actually doing—which was something I'd needed help seeing at the time—but we hadn't really gotten into why I was doing those things. Obviously, the "why" would come later for me as I started developing what would become The Way of the Quiet Warrior™. For me, though, that had been my first experience with a truly helpful and effective guide and losing her had felt like losing a limb. I suddenly felt so much less effective and everything seemed more difficult. I credit that as the first experience that really opened my eyes to the value of mentorship.

My situation was not unusual; many companies have recognized that their leaders are struggling and, to their credit, they have worked hard to integrate corporate coaches and mentors. However, those programs are only as good as the mentors provided and they only work when the CEOs are willing to engage with the coaches. I've worked with a lot of owner-operators who are running businesses that they built themselves or inherited from parents, and they often don't even have a board of directors, let alone a designated coach. The people who build these companies tend to be lone wolves who truly believe that they are better served by managing everything alone. After all, they started those companies as a team of one; why should they run the company any differently?

One thing that sets The Way of the Quiet Warrior™ apart from other coaching programs is that we not only recognize the distinct motives of our clients; we also actively integrate them into our plan. Our guides are trained to recognize the character of the person with whom we are working, and pinpoint the pitfalls that such people often experience, as well as their specific strengths.

For example, if we were working with a major Red personality, we would be aware of the fact that those folks are often resistant to being challenged and can be somewhat arrogant, making it difficult for them to see and acknowledge their mistakes. We would also be aware of the skills that person might have, including tenacity and stick-to-itiveness. Even the specific language that we use and the way we approach interactions would change depending on the motives of each personality involved. A Red leader, for example, would tolerate—even appreciate—a much more head-on approach, whereas a White leader would avoid anything that felt like conflict. Using all that information, our guides would be able to gently steer our client through The Way of the Quiet Warrior™ process toward his or her DMP by speaking the right language.

Our guides also know their own motives and personality profile, and share that with the client right up front. This enables each to understand how to work best with the other. For example, as a Blue guide, I tend to be more detail oriented and I approach relationships from the motive of intimacy. Developing personal relationships with others drives me. But if I am guiding a Red client, he or she wants me to be direct, to the point, and unemotional in my communication. The Red-Blue relationship is what we call "Fire and Ice"—a tricky but powerful combination—and without this unique understanding, such a partnership could easily fail. Our guides "speak four languages"—meaning, they have a full understanding of each major personality type—and that allows us to be more effective than any traditional mentoring program.

One exciting part of our program is our fruitful partnership with Dr. Taylor Hartman, which has allowed us to use his People Code and Character Code and even expand it in new ways. We have the world's first motive-based Character Profile tool, a "360-degree survey" that we offer to clients at the beginning of their journey. This survey not only helps us situate them in terms of their personality "colour" and core motive, but also gives them antidotes to their own limitations and a concrete way to mark their progress.

When we assess our clients' personality and character back in Phase One, THE SELF, we not only have them complete a self-assessment, but we also have them get significant people in their life to assess them as well (that's what the "360-degree" in the name refers to: a full, global view of the person). Then, at various critical stages, we have everyone complete the survey again to see if anything has changed and, if so, how it has changed. This gives us a very clear and concrete way of judging whether an individual is actually progressing or if he is stuck in his limitations. It also gives us a very clear tool to show someone just how far he might have come. This survey goes deeper than any other personality assessment I've ever encountered. It digs all the way down to our most hidden motivations, and I only wish I'd had this knowledge twenty years ago. It certainly would have saved me a lot of time and a lot of heartache.

No matter whom we are working with, however, guides in The Way of the Quiet Warrior™ have three primary utilities:

1. Accountability. This might be the best argument for having a guide in any aspect of your life. Having to answer to someone, even someone who is employed by you for that purpose, has an incredible psychological effect upon people. Accountability is a large part of why people hire personal trainers and tutors and instructors of all types: many of us require an external consequence to keep us on track.

If I know, for example, that I have a set meeting with a guide every week to debrief about my progress, that thought will be in my head throughout the week. I would feel not only a sense of working toward something specific, but also, a desire to succeed so I will have something positive to share with my guide. Similarly, if I began to wander away from the path, I wouldn't be able to wander too far because, at the end of the week, I would have an outside observer to reel me back in.

The great thing about the close working relationships that our guides develop with our clients is that the accountability goes both ways. I have a good friend named Ryan Walter who is a former NHL player from here in Canada, though he has played all over North America. I had a conversation with him once about how difficult it can be to stay on the path when your goal is akin to being successful in a major sport—a pursuit that involves an incredible amount of work and, to a large degree, luck as well.

He explained to me that two of the biggest factors that influence whether or not a player keeps progressing and moving forward are actually the atmosphere of the team around him and, most important, the attitude of the coach.

"I have been on teams where, if we lost a game, we blamed the ice, we blamed the crowd, we blamed our coach or our teammates, anything we could think of to avoid looking at our own performance. I have also been on Stanley Cup-winning teams—wildly successful teams—where we took responsibility for ourselves and our actions, where we looked at ourselves before looking for other places to cast blame. That attitude came from the top down and everyone on the team was accountable not just to their coach but also to their teammates and, most importantly, to themselves."

Today, Ryan actually has his own business and offers coaching services to people. He has also served as an athletic coach on several hockey teams. When he starts a mentorship-type relationship with anyone, however, he always asks him or her the same question: "Can you give me your permission to say that if you fail, *I* fail?"

It's a concept that he developed after many years of working on teams of all stripes. The best, most successful groups were always the ones in which the coach didn't just demand accountability and respect, but also offered it in return. The journey would be difficult, but it was easier in knowing that someone had thrown his lot in with yours. Someone now had a stake in your success.

With The Way of the Quiet Warrior™, I wanted to develop a system in which guides would truly invest in the people they were guiding. I wanted the success of the client to tie directly to the success of the guide, and the company overall. I wanted to be sure that our clients knew that we were beside them all the way.

2. Experience. Famed basketball player and coach John Wooden once said, "It's what you learn after you know it all that counts," and I've found that to be incredibly, almost painfully, true. There are a lot of things that we only really understand in retrospect and often it is through mistakes, wrong turns, and regrets that we learn the most important lessons.

Having a guide is an incredible way to sidestep some of the difficulty and wasted time in that process. Ideally, a guide should be someone with specialized knowledge, who, at the same time, has a broad base of experience from which to draw upon. In my own life, I've found that it's my varied experiences—and not just in my career—that have best enabled me to help people. If a person is having a problem in his or her business, it is almost never confined exclusively to the workplace. Nor are the roots of the problem just in his or her career choices. Family, career, physical health, personal history, it all comes together to create both problems and solutions, and a guide who can't empathize (and strategize) in all those areas can never be totally effective.

This is another one of the ways in which The Way of the Quiet Warrior™ (and KRE-AT™) is different from the myriad of other coaching services. Business coaches talk about business, fitness coaches talk about fitness, relationship coaches talk about relationships, and every one of them talks as though resolving this one area of your life will fix the rest of it. But at KRE-AT, we know that life is holistic, problems are holistic, and so our approaches to problem solving have to be holistic as well. The Way of the Quiet Warrior™ is designed to define purpose, take action, and create the life—the *whole* life—you want to live.

Part of the reason that so many people resist the idea of a coach or mentor is that they think that it means someone butting into their business and telling them what they "should" do. I, myself, had trouble with this before I discovered the motive-based character theory; someone could tell me to change my behavior all day, but unless he or she gave me a compelling reason why, I would drag my feet.

My personal model for guidance is very different. I'm not interested in telling people what they "should" do so much as I am in finding points of connection, times in my own life when I faced similar challenges, and explain what I did in those situations and how they worked out for me. I think of it as offering people additional data to help them make a decision, rather than instructing them on how they should act.

It's understandable, though, that many people would believe that guiding people actually means "telling them what to do." Most of us grew up learning almost everything via some authority figure telling us what to do and often not explaining *why* we should do it. In the corporate world, of course, offering quick and decisive solutions is heavily encouraged and it can be hard to break out of that didactic mode and simply share experiences.

Sharing experiences, though, is incredibly powerful. Not only does it go down easier with independent personalities, but it also helps to keep the relationship from becoming a one-sided teacher–student-type dynamic. In addition, it gives the advice-seeker more of a context for this advice. He can inquire for himself how specific courses of action worked out in other situations, rather than just hearing abstractions about the things he "needs" to do, with no idea what the result might be. It's also just a shorter, more concise, and more natural way to exchange ideas. When you get together with friends, do you want a PowerPoint presentation or just to swap stories?

I actually had a relevant experience recently. I was having a drink with a friend and the conversation drifted to our families. I brought up my daughter's summer vacation and how we were struggling a little bit with how to best use the time we had together. My daughter is very much a White personality, peace-loving and very indecisive, so it can be difficult to get a concrete plan out of her. We only had a few weeks before she had to head back up to school in Eastern Canada and I didn't want to waste that time trying unsuccessfully to pull together a trip or outing.

Immediately, my friend had all the solutions to my problems.

"Well, you should sit down with her, draw up a plan, and just make her stick with it, no matter what."

He sounded very confident so I asked him if this was something that he'd done with his own daughter.

"Oh," he said cheerfully, "I don't have kids."

I almost laughed. Here was a guy who had never been in this situation, but who was nevertheless convinced that he knew the one and only course of action that would get the results I wanted. I couldn't really take his advice seriously after that because I knew that, despite his confident tone, he had no real idea what would happen if I tried to strong-arm my daughter into making summer plans. I knew from my own experience with my daughter specifically, and White personalities in general, that it would be impossible. She wouldn't be strong-armed; she'd just retreat into herself and shut down, exactly what I *didn't* want to happen.

I would have been so much more responsive if someone had listened to my story and shared a story of his own. Maybe it would be a son instead of a daughter, or a spouse, or a parent; I didn't need the experiences to mirror each other exactly, but that person would in some way echo what I was seeing with my daughter. If he told me about the approach he took, how it made him feel, how it made the other person feel, and what actually happened as a result, I definitely would have taken that information to heart. It's true that I might not have done exactly what he did (and perhaps his story would be about how he forced the issue with his child and regretted it), but I would definitely use his story in my decision-making process. In that case, I could trust that my guide wasn't issuing blind instructions about a situation that he didn't really know much about; he was simply giving me counsel based on what he personally knew. Of course, no single guide would have experiences relevant to many situations, which is something we target in Phase Six, THE COMMUNITY.

Being able to pick someone else's brain in this way is also helpful in another practice that I've found very useful in my personal development: modeling behavior—or, to put it in simpler terms, copying. One of the most interesting things I got from Tony Robbins was the idea that, instead of trying to recreate success, look to someone who has been successful and copy his or her methods and behavior. One of my mentors once said, "Duplication is a four-syllable word for copy," and it has stuck with me all my life.

There is no need for us to reinvent the wheel if we have someone right in front of us offering examples of successful behavior. A guide won't just offer verbal shared experiences, but will serve as a template to follow, and, in that way, he or she is an incredible resource. A guide is there to be accountable, to help you move forward, and to make his or her experiences available to you. That is yours; take it.

3. Tracking and measuring progress. I mentioned that The Way of the Quiet Warrior™ has a specific system for gauging progress in terms of personality, particularly the core motive of "why" you do what you do, and character (which is simply developing strengths that aren't innate to you). The system also has a number of other tools designed to make it easy and effective for a client to see where he's going and how fast he's getting there.

Imagine that you are swimming an incredibly long distance in open water. There is no shore, no marker in sight, and every stroke feels just like the one before it. You can feel yourself becoming tired but, otherwise, you have no way of knowing how far you've come. As far as you're concerned, you might just be swimming in place.

Being midway through a major journey can feel a lot like that. A guide's job is to create a fixed marker that allows you, the client, to get a constant sense of where you are in relation to where you want to be.

The great thing about The Way of the Quiet Warrior™'s use of motive-based tools, like The People Code and The Character Code, is that every aspect of guidance can be geared toward the individual. That means that when we are developing ways to track progress, we will do that with the client's specific personality and motives in mind.

For example, as a Blue personality, I have to be wary about my tendency to allow anxiety to overwhelm me and cause me to shut down entirely. A single detail going awry can set me off on a chain of worry that might destroy my entire enterprise. I work best when I have an abundance of markers and a lot of smaller goals so that I don't become overwhelmed by the size of the task before my guide and I would know that. To return to the ocean metaphor, I need to have a buoy I can reach every few meters and I need to know there's a rescue boat following along side me.

A Red personality, by contrast, could swim and swim and swim with nothing in the way of tracking or reassurance, but he may very well swim way off track without noticing, or else push himself and others so hard that they all drown. In that case, it would be the guide's job to place pause points in his path and force him to take a moment for reflection and recalibration before diving back in again.

Every element of The Way of the Quiet Warrior™ was developed around the idea that we are helping unique individuals with specific motivations. We baked that idea into every phase, every tool, and every concept that we use. Everyone, no matter how skilled or successful, deserves—and occasionally requires—guidance tailored to him or her and his or her situation.

A single guide, however, can only take you so far. Real success requires more of a *team* effort.

THE BEND
IN THE RIVER

f it's that rope course again, I'm turning around and going home."

David had taken the window seat—he'd insisted—and Christa was crammed unhappily between him and Joanne Clarke, who had fallen into a deep sleep almost as soon as the plane had lifted off.

"I don't care if we're out in the middle of nowhere and I have to hike back to civilization," David continued, "I just can't face another year of zip-lining into my un-showered coworkers."

"It's not the rope course," Christa said quietly. "That place is further south, this is way up north."

"You know, I had a buddy, VP of this major bank, and his company had them all go down to Mexico and swim with sharks."

Christa suppressed an involuntary shudder. The idea of a murky, bottomless sea stretching out below her, full of all sorts of unknown terrors . . .

"There aren't any sharks in British Colombia," she said firmly.

"Well, we are bringing a plane full of executives up there. I imagine there's at least a couple of sharks on board right now," David grinned.

Christa leaned her head back against the seat and wished, not for the first time and certainly not for the last time, that she could sleep on planes.

———————

Their coordinator was an energetic woman named Jenn. She was wearing a fleece vest and had visible smears of sunscreen on her face. She clapped her hands to get their attention in a way that made Christa wonder if she typically dealt with school groups.

Jenn took them from the airport in a beat-up white van, bumping along over dirt roads until they reached what she called "the launch site." Out the window of the van, Christa could see a wide, seemingly placid river tumbling over rocks and the occasional fallen log.

Looking around the interior of the van, the others seemed to be regarding the river with everything from excitement (a young man whom Christa did not know by name) to revulsion (David, naturally).

"We're going to get into the water? In this weather?" He'd kept his voice to a mutter but Jenn had heard him all the same.

"Oh, we've got wet suits for you to keep you all nice and toasty."

Instead of comforting him, this only seemed to cause David more alarm.

"We're going to need wet suits?"

Christa couldn't resist: "Ropes course isn't looking so bad now, huh?" She was rewarded with a withering look.

———————

True to her word, Jenn provided them all with sturdy, if somewhat well-worn, wet suits and colourful life jackets as well. Christa allowed hers to dangle from her fingertips, feeling a cold that had nothing to do with the frigid temperature.

"But we aren't actually getting into the water, are we?" she asked, hating how tremulous her voice sounded, even to herself.

Jenn laughed.

"God, I hope not!"

"What's the matter, De Anza? Can't swim?" David teased, pulling his own life jacket on over the wet suit. His was a dull, sealskin grey.

"I can swim," Christa answered softly and, as she said it, it was almost like she could feel it again, the burning of the metal train tracks underneath her bare feet, her brother Jason's sweaty palm on her back, urging her closer and closer to the trestle's edge.

She had to "learn" is what he'd said. That's what he'd always said. She had to learn not to touch his stuff, so he'd dislocated her shoulder. She had to learn how to ride a bike, so he'd forced her down the big hill at the park and into a stand of trees. She had to learn not to swear at him, so he'd held her down and pushed dirt and grass into her mouth.

That day on the trestle, she'd had to learn to swim.

Christa had been so lost in the memory that she hadn't even noticed Jenn approach and place a comforting hand on her shoulder.

"Don't worry," Jenn said. "I'll be with you the whole time."

Christa forced a smile and shrugged on the life jacket. It felt not unlike the floaties she'd had to wear in her swim classes. Swim classes. That had been her family's only reaction to the train-trestle incident, exactly the sort of solution that solved nothing—typical of her parents. It was always easier for them to believe that Christa was in some way deficient than to wrestle with the idea that their golden firstborn might just be a psychopath.

In the case of swimming, though, Christa was deficient. On the first day of swim class, Christa had embarrassed herself almost immediately, choking, sputtering, and dropping like a stone to the bottom of the pool. After that, the instructor made her wear floaties; she was the only person in the class to have to do so. It was all the more frustrating because she had been able to float, to swim even, in the river underneath the train trestle, but in the peaceful, chlorinated sea of the local public pool, she floundered.

"OK!" Jenn clapped her hands again. "We're gonna hop in the rafts here on the shore and I'll hand you a paddle and show you some moves, all right?"

She held up a sleek, black paddle for emphasis. "We'll have you shooting rapids in no time!"

"Can't we just shoot actual shooters instead?" David grumbled.

They sat five to a raft. It was Christa; a silver-haired man whose name she thought might be "Trevor" or "Tanner"; an eager mid-forties woman, who had brought her own sleek, red-trimmed wetsuit; and, of course, David, who sat on the low bench right next to her. Almost as soon as they'd launched, there was already a thin layer of water in the raft, lapping around their feet.

Jenn was perched at the far end of the raft like a very dull ship's figurehead.

"We're going to go on a little ride, nothing too strenuous. Just use your paddles to kick off and get us moving."

They hardly had to push, as the water was moving much faster than Christa had guessed from looking at it earlier. It tugged eagerly at them, pulling them downstream and away from the launch site. Christa looked over her shoulder at the white van and one of the other river guides, who was cheerfully packing up the rest of their supplies.

"Hey," David gave her an indignant elbow, "you have to help paddle too!"

Christa turned forward again, dipping her paddle into the water. Her movements were awkward but the water helped her along, pulling the paddle back in a single fluid motion.

"Look at that," David marveled, pointing at a surge of foaming water ahead. "That must be the first rapid."

Christa felt something clench in her stomach like a knot pulled tight. The river underneath the train trestle had foamed and eddied in the same way. The shock of hitting the water had pushed almost everything out of her head, but, when she saw that white froth, she knew down in her bones that she had to get to the shore. If she allowed herself to be swept into that miniature maelstrom, she would drown.

And she didn't. Instead, she fought, kicking at the water and slapping it with her hands. It was the only thing she knew to do and, incredibly, it worked. She inched her way slowly, painfully over to the edge of the bank where, finally, she could touch the slick clay of the bottom with her toes. As she scrambled out of the river, she looked up to see her brother far up on the trestle watching her. It was too far away to see his exact facial expression but she knew from experience what it looked like: mildly interested, a little disappointed. Years later, when she was in high school, Christa finally got up the nerve to ask him why he had done it, and he just shrugged, saying, "I wanted to see what you would do."

They passed through the first rapid without major incident, just a slight bump and some spray that jetted over the side of the raft.

"You've got this!" Jenn enthused, her own paddle sitting inert across her thighs. Christa supposed it was meant just for emergencies. "Remember, sync your movements as much as you can. You're a team; gotta move like a team."

Christa glanced over at David and tried to match his slightly surer strokes but succeeded only in slamming his knuckles with the handle of her paddle.

"Sorry," she muttered.

David just shrugged.

"I can't feel my fingers anyway. I'll probably have frostbite by the end of this."

"I think they provide a campfire for us after we finish."

"I'd rather they provide a three-star-or-higher hotel for us—"

"OK," Jenn interrupted, "we're coming up on a bigger one; everyone get ready."

"Everyone get ready." The swim coach, a rangy old man with a mustache like a gray toothbrush laid lengthwise underneath his nose, roamed back and forth at the edge of the pool. Occasionally, he paused to adjust a student's position on the gritty black starting block. When he got to Christa, he gave her the kind of pitying look she'd grown used to getting from adults.

"Just do your best," he said, this time, in a quiet voice not intended to be overheard. Christa was grateful for that at least. He was, for all his gruff and bored appearance, a kindly sort.

"Everyone needs help sometimes," he told Christa when she struggled through the laps, fighting both the buoyancy of her floaties and her own panic response whenever the water splashed her face.

She finished the sprints in very last place, the rest of the class standing impatiently around the rim of the pool when she finally pulled herself, muscles quivering, out of the water.

"Great job," the instructor said, waiting until she was entirely out of the water to dismiss them. The other kids practically sprinted for the changing rooms, laughing and jostling one another.

To exactly no one's surprise, Christa had not managed to make any friends in her swim class.

"Hold on a minute there, Christa," her coach said, leading her over to a bench. The other floaties were stored there, underneath the seat, and Christa kicked at them idly as she waited for the coach to say something.

"This is your first year taking swim lessons, isn't it, Christa?"

She nodded, wary.

"And have you thought about what you're going to do when the school year starts?"

Christa gave him a blank look.

"What do you mean?"

"Are you considering joining the swim team?"

Christa was going into fifth grade—the first year in which kids could join the real sports teams, but she hadn't really given the idea much thought. She was an indoor kid and bad stuff tended to happen when she ventured too far away from the safety of her room—and the lock on the door.

"Not really," she said. "I'm not a good swimmer." The floaties, which kept her arms at an awkward angle to her body, squeaked as she shrugged her shoulders.

"No," the coach said easily. "But do you know that you are the only person who hasn't missed a single class this summer?"

Christa hadn't known that. Well, she *had* known that she hadn't missed a day; it was good to get away in the summertime, when Jason didn't have school to occupy him. He got bored easily and if she was around when he was feeling like making trouble . . . well, it was just better not to be around.

"OK . . ." she said, uncertain what this fact meant in terms of the swim team.

"You're not a natural in the water."

Christa thought that was putting it mildly.

"And you're scared of it."

Christa had known that it was probably obvious how little she liked being submerged in water, but it still sent a little spike of shame through her, hearing that the coach had noticed.

"But you come here every day and you get in the water and you do all your drills anyway. I can teach you to swim; I can't teach a kid dedication."

Christa nodded but, privately, she was thinking that her coach had it all wrong. She wasn't special; she wasn't more dedicated than anyone else. She just wanted to escape. She could feel the coach looking at her, trying to read something in her subdued reaction.

"You know," he said, his mouth quirking up into a smile, "I've had this mustache since I was fifteen years old, since I was old enough to grow it."

Christa looked up at him, completely bewildered. Now this was a conversation about facial hair?

"I grew it out to cover a scar I have on my lip. You see, when I was a little kid, I got bitten by a dog. They didn't have all the cosmetic surgery stuff back then so it healed a little ugly."

Christa still couldn't figure out why he was telling her this but she sat and listened politely, just the same.

"It wasn't even one of the scary breeds, you know, like a Rottweiler or a pit bull. It was just a little thing, a beagle mix. I must have antagonized it somehow because it lunged right at me and snapped, caught my upper lip and part of my nose. I was about four years old and, after that, I was terrified of dogs. If I even saw a dog on a leash, I'd cross the street or hide behind my parents to avoid it.

"My dad decided that he'd had enough of that when I was about your age and so, one day, I came home from school to find that he'd brought home this little-bitty rat-dog: a Chihuahua, and the runt of the litter, at that. Full grown, and the creature weighed about three pounds. My dad told me it would be ridiculous to be scared of a little thing like that, and I had to admit that he was right.

"But I still didn't like him. I avoided him at first but he was curious about me, started following me around, trying to get me to pet him. He had these real long legs and he walked funny, like a man on stilts. Once in a while, I'd leave a little bit of food on the floor and let him take it. From there, I worked up to feeding him from my hand. He barely had teeth to speak of, more like tiny pebbles than anything else. Even if he had bitten me, it probably wouldn't have broken the skin.

"And, just like that, I got used to him. I could feed him and pet him and even let him sit in my lap sometimes. After a while, I started to get a little better about dogs. I still wasn't crazy about the big ones, but I could manage, you know?"

Christa nodded because she *did* know and, on her way out of the pool that day, she paused at the front desk to pick up the forms required to try out for the swim team.

This part of the river was much rougher and Jenn was barking directions in a steady voice that carried over the sound of the water and of Christa's raft mates exclaiming at every bump and jostle.

"Paddle right!" she shouted, and Christa dug her paddle into the river on her right. It moved awkwardly and she thought she felt it hit something solid. There were rocks all over here in the river, emerging in jagged peaks and pebbly piles from the eddying water. Christa wondered how deep it was here but she knew that it didn't matter. With a current like this, if she fell out, she'd be swept along before she would even have time to try to swim for shore.

"Crap!" David shouted and Christa followed his line of vision to see an enormous rock, more like a wall than anything else, rising up to meet them about forty yards ahead. Christa could feel her eyes widening and she could hear the sudden roar of blood in her ears. There was no way they weren't going to hit that rock; there was nowhere else to go. She could see it in her mind's eye: the little raft careening off the rock, the impact flipping the craft and dumping them into the water. Panic, confusion, hands scrambling for any kind of purchase. If the river didn't drown them, their raft mates would.

Christa realized she wasn't moving. Her hands were tight and motionless on the paddle, which was dragging uselessly in the water. Somehow, Jenn found her and caught her gaze. Jenn smiled and Christa couldn't help but be reminded of her swim coach and how, sometimes, when she was struggling through another set of laps, she would look over and find him giving her an encouraging smile.

"Paddle left!" Jenn shouted then and Christa could feel the hesitation in the air. Paddling left would put them on a direct course toward the enormous rock. "Now!" Jenn insisted and, almost automatically, Christa began paddling as hard as she could manage.

She tensed, waiting for Jenn to tell them to turn aside. The rock was coming up fast now and surely she was going to have them turn, do some fancy maneuver to dart around the impassible formation.

"Don't close your eyes!" Jenn said and Christa realized that she had, in fact, done just that.

Her eyes flew open. The rock was just ahead of them. There was no fancy maneuver; there was no turning aside. They were going to hit that rock formation and there was nothing she could do to stop it.

Again, she felt the blaze of the hot train tracks under her bare feet, Jason's insistent pushes at her back. The edge of trestle crept closer and closer. She was going to fall and there was nothing she could do to stop it.

The raft hit on the side and banked sharply up in the air. Christa heard a distant "whoa!" as the occupants of the raft were lifted from their seats. For a moment, they were floating and then they came back down hard onto the seats in the raft, which was somehow gliding smoothly along on the unobstructed river.

There was a bend in the river, narrow and practically invisible from the other side. To get to it, the raft had to skim off the big rock formation—

had to strike it head-on. Jenn must have known that. She probably knew this stretch of the river like the back of her hand; she could guide a raft around that rock in her sleep. Christa looked over her shoulder again to watch the formation as it passed. It was covered in sharp protrusions and hard angles, striking it at almost any angle would likely mean tearing the raft itself. Christa tried to calculate the percentage of rock that they could safely bump up against; it had to be small.

"OK," Jenn chirruped, "let's bring 'er back to shore!"

Back at the campsite, they made hot cocoa for the whole team, with actual melted chocolate in a small metal pot. David was huddled as close as possible to the fire, griping to anyone who would listen about his probable case of frostbite. Christa sat beside him, thoughtfully sipping her drink.

"You did a good job out there," Jenn said, flopping down beside her. "Good teamwork."

"It was all you." Christa replied. "You knew all the turns to make."

Jenn shrugged.

"Sure, you had some help, but you're the ones who did it. My paddle never touched the water."

Christa gave her a small smile.

"Well, thank you for your help."

Jenn reached forward to poke at the fire with a stick. A spiral of sparks shot up into the air. It was coming on sunset now and Christa could see her breath in the air, but, somehow, she didn't mind the cold.

"That's a river guide's job, ma'am," Jenn said cheerfully. "We're here to help you get where you're going."

6

PHASE SIX
THE COMMUNITY

What is the secret to long-term success?
What keeps you growing?

There is a well-known phrase usually applied to education and child-rearing: "It takes a village to raise a child." In my opinion, though, that sentiment doesn't just apply to child-rearing. It takes a community to create a Warrior.

Not only is a warrior more vulnerable on his or her own; a warrior without a community has nothing to fight for and nowhere to go when the battle is over. Close your eyes and imagine that you are in a space—virtual or literal, it doesn't matter—and you are sharing that space with amazing people. People who are like you, who share your values and your desires, and they are warriors like you. You have all come together in this place to find harmony and to turn your purpose into a reality. This is an inviting and secure place, a place where all motives are known and all languages are spoken. Here, you can truly communicate and truly be understood. Welcome to the community.

Welcome to your tribe.

Napoleon Hill calls it a "mastermind alliance." Mental-health professionals call it a "support group." In the corporate world, it is often simply called a "peer group." But whatever the name, no one discounts to the value of a group of like-minded people working together in harmony toward a common purpose.

Nothing of real significance gets accomplished via one person acting alone. Even the creation of this book required the combined efforts of editors, graphic designers, publishers, and printers, and that's not even mentioning the incredible help and support I received from people in my life while I was working on it.

Human beings gravitate toward communities and that's why The Way of the Quiet Warrior™ mimics the same structure of human society-building. We start with the individual and work up from there to building connections—at first, with one or two individuals, and finally, with a tribe of warriors. A Way of the Quiet Warrior™ tribe is a Hill-style mastermind alliance, a tightly knit group of high-achievers and lifetime learners in sync with one another and working toward a purpose.

Phases One through Five of The Way of the Quiet Warrior™ are designed to prepare you to create and maintain a positive community that will help you reach your DMP goals and keep you on track toward your purpose. By the time you reach Phase Six, you should have everything you need to build a truly positive network of support.

Obviously, not all communities are created equal, and there are toxic communities out there. I've worked with several tribes that were deeply sick in terms of their interpersonal dynamics. Often, this was a top-down problem that began with a leader who was engaging in toxic leadership behaviors, but I've also encountered groups that were unproductive and unhealthy for other reasons. Size, for example, has a large bearing on how agile and effective a community can be. When a community grows too large, it can be very difficult to achieve harmony and singleness of purpose, which are the most important parts of a good, effective team. For that reason, I like to keep my communities relatively small. Doing so also allows me to check in regularly with all the members and make sure they are on track and aren't falling into negative behaviors or modes of thinking.

One of the most important aspects of a community, in terms of manifesting one's purpose, is the peer relationship. Unlike a guide, your community should be made up of people who are more or less in the same boat as you are, and who are working in harmony toward a common purpose. Being able to find common ground with someone is the beginning of rapport and trust, which is a critical component of our tribes. Only when we feel comfortable showing vulnerability can we really put aside our egos—often a problem, especially when working with highly successful people.

Creating a tribe of similar people also allows us to share the triumphs and challenges of navigating our path with people who are facing the same things. Alcoholics Anonymous, for example, is a globally successful "tribe" based around the shared experience of alcohol addiction. When my father finally decided to quit drinking, AA helped him, as it has done for many others. Part of AA's efficacy is the fact that it allows alcoholics to forge connections with people who are struggling with the same demons.

Similarly, I chair a board for a nonprofit called the Mood Disorders Association of BC, and I've been working with that group for eight years now. They provide a variety of support services for people struggling with mental illness—everything ranging from depression and anxiety to bipolar disorder and schizophrenia. One aspect of that support comes in the form of smaller peer groups, which are composed of, and led by, volunteers. Often, these volunteers will be people who are living with the same issues that the group is designed to address. So, for example, if you were looking for a support group for depressive disorders, you could expect that group to be led by someone who has personal experience with depression. This ethos is a critical part of the organization as a whole; no matter what arm of the nonprofit, you can expect to find people who are either living with mental illness or are personally affected by it. This creates a sense that we are all in the same struggle together; there aren't leaders or followers, just people with some problems in common, trying to help one another and sharing a common purpose.

But this concept works for more than just mental health. I also have been doing a lot of work lately with an organization called MacKay CEO Forums, which is designed to create forums or peer groups for CEOs and executives. The "MacKay" in its name refers to Dr. Nancy MacKay, who observed many of the same problems I did in the corporate world with executives who were feeling isolated and myopic. Her vision is to "populate the world with better leaders" and one of the most important ways she does that is via peer groups.

The groups are small—eight to fourteen CEOs and executives—and we try to find people who are roughly analogous with one another in terms of their responsibilities and career level. We gather the groups together periodically, and essentially, spend a day in conversation. It's a little bit war room, a little bit therapist's office, but we all gather in a boardroom and just work through the issues and problems we are experiencing.

We brainstorm and share experiences, working out strategies and solutions, but we also offer a space where people can simply vent about things they are facing in both their personal and professional life. Everyone gets an opportunity to speak and the rest of the group can respond constructively and offer shared experiences or commiseration. Napoleon Hill calls this sort of group discussion "masterminding," which merely means that two or more smart people are putting their heads together and collectively solving problems that stymied individual members.

With the right structures in place, groups of people can be the best problem solvers and information aggregators in the world. The Internet age has proven this to us again and again. It's why your smartest friend can't tell you as much about as many things as the user-generated Wikipedia. It's why there are no "surprises" anymore in serialized storytelling; with millions of people watching every week and thinking through every possible permutation of narrative, someone always figures out whodunnit and why before a show, book, or movie ends. There *is* wisdom in crowds; we just have to figure out how to harness it productively.

Peer groups are an established part of many industries and many systems of leadership development. During my time in the corporate world, I've been a member of dozens—if not hundreds—of teams and groups, but the difference in community building within The Way of the Quiet Warrior™ is the same as we bring to every other aspect of this journey: a focus on individual motivation.

Groups coming together to find solutions are a tool in the way blueprints are a tool. Just as with the blueprint, The Way of the Quiet Warrior™ takes an existing tool and infuses it with all the foundational ideas of motivation; character; and deep, driving purpose. Different groups are right for meeting needs, and the tribes that we build with The Way of the Quiet Warrior™ are specifically designed to help move our clients down the path toward fulfilling their ultimate purpose.

Most groups are not set up with the goal of recognizing or working with individual motivations, and they often take a "one size fits all" approach. This can create problems both small and large because, inevitably, the structure of the group will not work for everyone. For example, when I was working as a manager and executive, I was nearly always part of a group assigned to specific projects. Whenever we met, we would usually open with a call to address issues and problems, and then we'd allow the entire room to put forth solutions or share relevant information. This is a sensible structure that works for many personality types, but not all of them.

I've found that Red personalities will often jump right in and lead the discussion, which is great. The challenge there is making sure that the Red people in the room don't monopolize the conversation. Personally, I like to make sure that people keep their contributions rooted in their own experience. As we discussed in Phase Five, I find it so much more effective when someone tells you about a similar situation he or she had and how it was resolved, rather than just issuing instructions. Red personalities, however, with their decisiveness and efficiency, often default into simply telling people what to do.

On the other end of the spectrum, you might have on a team some White personalities, who would really struggle with sharing openly in front of a group at all. People with White personalities tend to fade into the background, especially when there are more flashy personalities taking up all the air in the room.

Obviously, the situation wouldn't be ideal for anyone. Your White team member may have amazing ideas that never get heard, while your Red team member may be charging ahead without really understanding the problem on the table, and nothing would get resolved.

Just as having conflicting personalities on a team can lead to problems, having too many similar personalities can also lead to a toxic environment. A team composed entirely of Yellow personalities would probably have a thousand different ideas, but would be unable to follow through with any of them, while a team of Blues may very well create an echo chamber of worry, in which they only amplify one another's fears about the project.

The Way of the Quiet Warrior™ strives to create mastermind alliances of people who connect with one another and strive for the same purpose—our tribes. We don't want to simply lump people together based on proximity or industry, but actually bring people together thoughtfully because they are truly complementary personalities with an ability to work together in harmony.

All personalities benefit from positive communities. The independent Reds often require a voice of caution and someone to help them manage the small details that they are prone to overlooking. Anxious Blues thrive when they have a group of people to go to when they need certainty and decisive action during a difficult project. Non-confrontational Whites can use the support of others to make hard decisions that they might otherwise avoid. Finally, the freewheeling and enthusiastic Yellow personalities are much more successful when they have people around them to keep them on task and help them channel their incredible energy in a productive way.

This doesn't necessarily mean that every tribe should be composed of one of each personality type. Most people have strengths and limitations of more than one type, for example, so our guides will use the tools we established in earlier phases to develop a kind of portrait of each client. With that information, we can bring people together in the ways that seem likeliest to benefit everyone.

This also allows us to do much more effective conflict resolution in those groups. Our guides can speak all the languages and can occasionally step in as "interpreters" to help facilitate communication between members of the tribe. At the same time, we will also work toward teaching our clients the skills that they need to create and maintain positive tribes, and that is something they can apply to any community—any relationship, even—in their lives.

We want to ensure that these communities will continue to be fruitful and healthy as we move further along toward realizing our purpose. That is why everyone who joins a tribe—or enters a mastermind—creates a Mastermind-Alliance Statement (or "MMA Statement"). Basically, this is just a set of guidelines that everyone in the tribe can agree upon, ground rules, if you will.

Each MMA Statement will be geared toward the tribe as a whole and designed to help further whatever purpose goals the individual members have. If I were forming a tribe of people who were trying to advance toward their purpose, for example, one of the points in my MMA Statement would be something like, *We will all share our DMPs with one another.* That allows us to have a sense of what each person is working toward, and we can use that information to offer better solutions.

Another common element of these statements is an agreement that the tribe is in harmony, and that if someone falls out of harmony, he or she is no longer in the mastermind. This is a key point because if you introduce a lot of conflict into a small tribe, the situation can go bad very quickly. Negative ways of thinking—those weeds in the subconscious that we discussed—can get out of hand in a small group. We have to create a new reality within our tribes, a place without the negative thinking that will bog us down and keep us from meeting our goals. For example, one of my goals last year was to lose thirty pounds—and I did, indeed, do that—but part of what I needed to do to make that happen was banish negative thoughts about my body. If I indulged in self-hatred or self-pity, I was only going to put up barriers between myself and my goals. Part of eliminating those thoughts meant avoiding people who were vocally negative about their bodies, my body, or the bodies of strangers. Their words would stick in my subconscious just as deeply as my own, if I allowed it.

Even—sometimes, *especially*—if it's only one member of the group creating issues, it can devolve rapidly. I have seen otherwise-successful communities contort themselves in trying to make one toxic individual fit in successfully, and it never works. This is because, typically, the problem is not with the group and the group cannot fix the individual; only he or she can do that. My very Red client whom I had to fire was a great example of this. In his case, it would have been very difficult to remove him from the mastermind (as he was the boss and all), but his negative behaviors and unyielding personality were making it impossible for the team to function, no matter how hard they tried to accommodate him.

Most people also include logistical details in the MMA statement, nailing down when the group will meet and under what circumstances. This is also highly tailored to the tribe in question. Some people can meet every weekend at the local coffee shop, while others can only connect via conference call or video chat. A virtual community is no longer a futuristic concept and The Way of the Quiet Warrior™ has incorporated this facet of modern life. I expect that we will only see more of this virtual community building as we move forward; few demographics have as enthusiastically embraced communal bonding and guides in the way millennials have, and we are already seeing more and more workflow applications designed to help people collaborate from afar.

One of the other major components of a mastermind-alliance agreement is trust. We want to establish a confidential relationship between peers so everyone involved feels comfortable sharing openly without fear that others in the mastermind are going to repeat sensitive information. People who are leading large companies or who are engaged in other high-profile careers can naturally be quite wary of baring their soul to strangers. This can lead to people being cagey and uncommunicative, so we try to avoid that in the beginning by establishing strict disclosure rules for everyone in the tribe.

Many CEOs, business owners, and others in leadership positions are used to keeping everything inside. If they are feeling fear, frustration, or virtually any other negative emotion, they can't exactly go to their board of directors and talk through those feelings (if they even have a board!). Leaders are often called upon to project an air of invincibility, and, for many people, the pressures of maintaining that facade can be overwhelming. Of course, some people cope with this by going home and hashing out their problems with their families or with friends, but those listeners generally don't have direct experience with their situation. Being able to vent to people who not only understand what you're experiencing, but also know your core motives and your purpose—and can offer their own insights gleaned from personal experience—is incredibly powerful.

Just as with the concept of guides, many people who have never had a resource like that can't fully understand how much it adds to one's life. It's hard to completely comprehend that without experiencing it firsthand, and part of The Way of the Quiet Warrior™ is easing people into this process, which may be new or uncomfortable for them. I have found, though, that once people actually get involved in a good, effective mastermind, they can't go back to doing everything on their own. It feels like suddenly having to drive a car without a steering wheel.

The overall goal of Phase Six of The Way of the Quiet Warrior™ is the same goal of every other phase: to move you forward with continuous motion. We are continuing to eat that elephant one bite at a time, and elements like the guide system and the peer groups are designed to help the client keep going, even when it's difficult. The purpose is big and the road might be very long. Most of us are going to have moments of exhaustion or doubt. That is when we need others to keep us on track and to diffuse a little bit of the burden, or even to offer up a fresh solution that we hadn't considered.

The first time I really engaged with a great tribe of people was during one of the more difficult periods in my life. I was still working as a temporary CEO for companies that needed resuscitation. I was working all the time and my health was eroding by the day. To top it off, I had married Anna not that long before, and we had also just weathered the loss of a child. Anna's ex-husband was an additional strain on the family, drawing out their divorce and custody proceedings and adding constant strife whenever we had to interact with him—which, for the sake of the boys, was fairly frequently.

To say that I was under pressure would be putting it mildly. I was dying, and I mean that quite literally. My doctor told me that, if I continued on in that way, I would give myself a heart attack or stroke, probably sooner rather than later.

When a friend of mine called me with an opportunity to join a peer group, I was skeptical at first. I'd never heard of anyone doing anything like that, and I thought at first that it was some sort of scam because the group did require an entry fee.

My friend convinced me to give it a try, however, describing it as "a group of people who get together and solve problems." At that time in my life, I was desperately in need of some problem solving and I was willing to try something unorthodox.

Despite all that, I went into the group with no real expectations. I had no idea what I was going to find or if I'd ever go back to another meeting. As it turned out, I spent seven years in that group, and they helped me navigate one of the most challenging times in my life. This was my first real exposure to being in a mastermind and it was amazing. To put it politely, they helped me get my life in order. To put it less politely, they kicked my ass. Over the course of those seven years, my career, my marriage, my health, and my net worth all grew and were considerably strengthened.

The first thing I really responded to was the consistency and accountability built into the format. I knew that I would be meeting with these people every month, so I also knew that if I set a goal or made a statement one week, they were going to expect some sort of follow-up the next week. This worked for commitments in every aspect of my life. If I told them that I was going to take my executive team for an off-site planning session to deal with a sales problem, I knew I was going to need to tell them how that planning session went the next time I saw them. If I said that I was going to start running to improve my health, they were going to want to know how many miles I'd managed. If I didn't have anything to report, I knew that I would be facing the disappointment and censure of the group, and that really helped keep me on track.

As I settled in with the group, I began to seek counsel on things that weren't directly related to work, and I found that many other people in the group had gone through similar things. I was struggling at that time with how to help Anna with her ex-husband. I found it difficult to fully understand her position because my own divorce had been sad but very amicable. I had no experience dealing with a partner who was actively trying to harm me. Several people in the group *had* had that experience, however, and listening to their stories helped me put our situation in context and gave me some solutions to try.

I don't know how long I could have lasted if I didn't find that group. Keeping everything inside and pushing myself further and further was never going to be a long-term solution, but I didn't have the tools to do anything else. Joining a community of like-minded people allowed me to develop those tools. In retrospect, I know now that this group was amazing in many ways, but it didn't completely meet my needs. I worked toward goals but they had no true purpose behind them. I found success but happiness eluded me. I knew that community was important and I believed that I could find something—or make something—that would give me exactly the right type of tribe to call my own.

Since then, I've actively sought out other communities and I continue to get a lot of value from them. Every community is different and they have all taught me important lessons that I've since incorporated into The Way of the Quiet Warrior™. For example, one thing that I took from my experiences in various groups was the practice of having a short debrief (often called a "five-minute huddle") with the tribe before beginning a workday. This is, essentially, a mini-mastermind session in which everyone can quickly check in and bring up his or her top three focuses for the day, as well as any pertinent issues that he or she has before the group scatters. It's amazing what a difference in productivity this simple practice can create. When people have the opportunity to clearly state where they are, both in terms of practical progress and emotionally, and also hear where their teammates are, they go into their day with a new confidence. This is something that I recommend to almost anyone in a leadership position.

Another excellent tactic for getting perspective on your journey is the laser call. This is something that groups do in addition to the standard meeting, often on a daily basis. You simply call up your group members, and then you each have one minute to list three things you are grateful for. You then each tell the others where your focus is going to be for the day, and then you're done. There's no additional conversation; that is reserved for the full meetings. The laser call is designed to fill your mind with positive thoughts and gratitude—fuel for your subconscious. It is designed to get you thinking about where you are and where you're going, something that can be hard to remember when you're working toward a goal that may take years to realize. Too often, we can slip into autopilot and start doing things just because they are what we've always done. Techniques like the laser call force us to stop and meditate for a moment on positive ideas, seeds that will eventually bear wonderful fruit. When you multiply those ideas by the number of people on the call, it adds up to something incredibly powerful.

When we talk about tribes, however, we also have to talk about the difficult reality that not everyone in a given group is going to succeed. If we return to Napoleon Hill's estimate that only 5 percent of people actually figure out their true purpose, and only a small fraction of that 5 percent of people realize their purpose, we have to assume that some—perhaps many—of the individuals you encounter in peer groups will fall off the path for one reason or another. The Way of the Quiet Warrior™ has been designed to dramatically increase the probability of success, and our tribes are set up to keep everyone moving forward on their journeys.

I have seen firsthand what happens when groups begin to disintegrate. When a group I worked with started doing the daily laser call, there were about eight people on the call every day. Slowly, over the course of a few weeks, people started falling away. Some of them felt they couldn't commit the time anymore. Some of them decided that that whole mastermind process wasn't for them. Some of them became disillusioned. Some of them decided they weren't going to make it. They all had their reasons. In the end, it was just myself and two other people. The attrition rate is significant. Most of those who fall off the path don't have the benefit of a clear DMP backed by some burning desire.

But do you know where else the attrition rate is significant? In athletics. How many people did you know growing up who had a talent for basketball or swimming or tennis? And how many of those people went on to play those sports at a very high level? How many even still play casually? I would guess that number is very small indeed.

If you think about those special few who do go on to incredible achievements, they generally have a few things in common. Many have a positive mental attitude, single-minded focus, and a defined purpose that won't let them quit—something that they may have even developed as a young child. They also have a blueprint of clearly defined goals and specific actions that they need to accomplish according to a predetermined schedule. Perhaps most important, they have an extended network of supporters: coaches, family, coworkers, teachers, medical professionals, and numerous others.

These people aren't inherently better than the kid you knew who was really, really good at track, and they don't know a secret that the rest of us don't. Instead, they simply felt their purpose calling to them and decided to answer that call to adventure. Along the way, they utilized every tool at their disposal to get closer to fulfilling that purpose and they weren't afraid to lean on others.

The Way of the Quiet Warrior™ is designed to streamline this process: to give people a plan and help them at every stage of that plan. Many people only manifest their purpose after years of painful trial and error, reinventing the wheel at every turn. That is why I collected everything I'd learned, everything I had gleaned from others who had suffered and strived for years, and built a system that would streamline that process and avoid all the unnecessary hardship. THE SELF, THE VISION, THE PATH, THE BLUEPRINT, THE LAUNCH, and THE COMMUNITY is the only motive-based program that guarantees success for those who want it.

The Way of the Quiet Warrior™ is a community unto itself, a network of people from all over the planet dedicated to helping you find and fulfill your true purpose. The odds of manifesting the dreams that drive us are small, but those odds are increased when we band together and pool our intellectual and emotional resources. After all, it does take a community to create a warrior—and it takes a tribe to sustain one.

FAMILY TREE

It started in the car from the airport. The driver, a taciturn man with a blond buzz cut, kept looking back in the rearview mirror and John could see his worried eyes reflected there.

"Sir?" the driver said finally, when they were about half a mile from the hotel itself. "Are you OK?"

"Yup," John managed, his voice a painful croak. He hadn't worn a tie but he still felt like there was something around his neck, tightening incrementally but indomitably. When they pulled up in front of the hotel's big revolving door, John left his suitcase in the back of the car as he staggered toward the front desk.

"Wait!" the driver called, jogging after him with the suitcase.

The man gave him a searching, worried look and John could tell that he was working himself up to asking about John's health again.

"Thanks," John gasped, practically yanking the suitcase from the driver's hands and dashing into the hotel.

John could feel sweat creeping down his cheeks and the back of his neck as the girl behind the front desk checked him in over the course of what felt like hours, but was probably only about five minutes.

Get to the room, John told himself in the calmest mental voice he could muster. *The room, the room, the room, theroomtheroomtheroom . . .* He zombie-staggered to and from the elevator. His room was room 404 and he had the absurd thought that his Chinese grandmother would have refused to stay there, four being an unlucky number. He wondered if his daughter would have asked for another room as well. She was only a quarter Chinese but she was all millennial, and she probably wouldn't want to stay in the "Error: Page Not Found" room either.

The room didn't feel unlucky to John, though. When he stepped inside, it was like walking into a wall of cool air. He felt himself relax, the invisible thing around his throat slackened ever so slightly.

John draped himself across the bed, not even bothering to stow his suitcase or take off his shoes. The smooth, synthetic bedspread was oddly soothing against his face. When he turned his head, he could hear it prickle and catch on his five-o'clock shadow. He laid there for a long time, breathing slowly and evenly, and squeezing his eyes shut as tightly as he could manage.

It seemed that he could feel his pulse in every part of his body. It was throbbing in his throat, his wrists, his stomach, and his temples. It was ticking away like a clock, too fast, he thought. Much faster than it should have been going. He wondered if that was a symptom of a heart attack, feeling your pulse jump wildly. He imagined his heart, looking like the images he'd seen in health class years ago. He imagined each of the chambers shivering as they struggled to pump blood as quickly as the rest of his body demanded it.

What happened to a heart that beat too fast? Did it just become exhausted and slow to a crawl before finally stopping? Or did it burst like an over-ripened fruit, splattering his insides with . . . more of his insides?

John reached up blindly, groping for the telephone on the nearby end table. He was relieved to discover that this was one of those hotels where the phone connected automatically to the front desk. He pressed the cool plastic against his ear and heard the familiar, neutral tone of the woman at the front desk.

"I think . . . I think I need a doctor," John managed before letting the phone slide into the space between his face and neck. The woman at the front desk was talking but he couldn't hear her. Instead, her voice was a distant buzzing against his skin, a blurry counterpoint to the overwhelming throb of blood in his ears.

———————

"Panic attack," said the cheerful EMT who seemed way too young for his job. Surely he couldn't be much older than John's daughter. John couldn't imagine his little girl elbow-deep in other people's blood and guts all day. Not that John was spilling any blood.

"You're gonna be my easiest call all day," the EMT assured him.

"Panic attack," echoed the harried doctor, a petite black-haired woman with heavy purple shadows under her eyes. She kept look nervously at the door behind John during his exam, and he could tell that she was itching to get back to her other patients—her *real* patients.

"This should help with the panic attacks," said the staff psychiatrist, tearing a sheet off his prescription pad and holding it out to John.

"Panic *attack*," John corrected softly. "It only happened that one time."

The psychiatrist said nothing and just stared, unblinking, until John leaned forward and took the paper from his hand.

"How are you feeling, Mr. Zhao?" asked the woman at the front desk. Her voice was still full of that same impersonal faux-warmth but her eyes were very soft. Maybe it was her eyes that made John lean heavily on the check-in desk and tell her the truth.

"Not so good," he said. "It felt like I was going to die."

She nodded sympathetically.

"I used to get panic attacks all the time in college. It always felt like dying, no matter how many times it happened."

No matter how many times it happened. The idea of feeling like that again, multiple times even, sent a cold shock of fear through John. He cleared his throat awkwardly.

"Did any calls come in for me?"

"Yes, your wife called, but when they were loading you into the ambulance, you requested that we not disclose any information to your family, so I just told her you were unavailable." The woman's eyebrows knit together in worry. "You were . . . a little out of it, though. If that wasn't what you wanted, I apol—"

"No, no," John assured her, "you did exactly right." Cherie didn't need another reason to resent his constant business travel. "I'll call her from the room. Thanks."

John paused a moment, looking at the front-desk girl and her placid, immaculate smile. She looked young; college could not have been that long ago for her.

"You said you used to have those . . . those attacks," John began hesitantly. "What made them stop?"

The girl flushed slightly and laughed.

"Well, I'm not sure if it's something that would work for everyone. I'm kind of a hippie."

Looking at her with her neat French braid, her starched and pressed exterior, John found that hard to believe.

"What is it?"

"It's a sort of . . . natural medicine, I guess you'd call it. There's a woman here in the city that I go and see. She gives me recommendations: herbal treatments and some physical therapies. After I started seeing her, I noticed a lot of improvement."

John thought about the paper sack of anonymous pills in his jacket pocket.

"Does she have a card or something?" he asked and the woman nodded eagerly, scrawling something on a slip of paper.

"Her office is in Chinatown," she said. "She's a little old-school, so it's probably better just to go there in person." The girl paused and gave him an appraising sort of look. "I think she'll like you."

The interior of the shop smelled familiar, though John could not identify all of the components of the smell. Ginger, definitely, and the dull sweetness of mānuka honey, but lots of other things as well. He recognized just a few of the products that lined the walls in small glass containers, neatly labeled in both English and Mandarin. He had seen his grandmother cook with some of these things, like the dried black mushrooms with their softly crinkled edges or the white lotus seeds that looked like the goggly eyes of a doll. Other things—some powdered, some dried, some damp and glistening—were entirely new to him.

When he rang the silver bell next to the ancient cash register, no one immediately appeared, so he circled the room slowly, perusing the wares. Some of the containers had small descriptions; this one was supposed to be good for constipation—that one, for memory. There were lots for digestion. John had a brief flash of his grandmother clucking her tongue at him for drinking ice water with his dinner. "Warm is better for digestion!" she had scolded.

The old woman emerged from the back apologizing, a canvas apron tied around her waist. She was younger than John had expected, maybe in her fifties or early sixties, and her short hair was black as a crow's wing. She smiled when she saw John.

"Hello! You want a consult?"

John was momentarily thrown. Did he want a consult?

"I've been having some . . . problems with anxiety," he said, hoping that answered her question.

She nodded as though this were something she had expected to hear from him and gestured toward the back of the shop, hidden behind a dull-green cloth curtain.

"Come along then, háizi," she said.

Háizi. It had been a very long time since anyone had called him "child." That was something he recalled from the six weeks he spent visiting his grandmother in China during his gap year: the familiar forms of address that made a great, universal family from countless strangers. It was a country of more than a billion people but every older woman was an auntie and every older man an uncle. Young folks were liberally addressed as "little sister," "little boy," or, as the old woman called him, simply "child."

He'd never quite gotten the hang of the practice and he was unsure now if he was supposed to respond in kind. He'd forgotten the word for "madam," which would have been more formal, but he knew the term for "auntie."

"Thank you…āyí," he tried.

The old woman seemed to accept that, turning and vanishing behind the curtain. John followed her.

"Nervous," she said when he stepped into the back room, which was small and featured a number of soft leather chairs, more of those glass containers of herbs, and a large fish tank. "Anxious and unhappy." It was not a question.

"The doctor said I had a panic attack. It felt like my heart was . . . going into overdrive," John offered.

The old woman gestured for him to sit down and then took a seat opposite him.

"They gave you medication? To manage the symptoms?"

John nodded.

"It can help," she said, as though John had questioned the pills' efficacy. Perhaps she could see something of the doubt that thus far had kept him from removing the prescription bottle from its paper sack. "But it is not everything. Your brain does not stand alone; everything in the body is connected. To resolve your anxiety, you must treat the whole body, the whole life. Sit forward."

Without thinking, John obeyed her and she began feeling around his abdomen and back.

"Hmm . . . pàng," she murmured and, off of John's bewildered look, clarified: "You are carrying extra weight."

John bit back a nasty response. He knew he wasn't in the best shape but he worked seventy hours a week and spent a lot of that time flying from one city to the next. It didn't leave a lot of time for cardio.

"Do you drink?" she asked, pressing deeper into his side. It was becoming almost painful.

"Socially," he said and she made another *hmm* sound. The sheer number of after-hours negotiations and relationship-building sessions that went on in various hotel bars meant that he couldn't just abstain. He'd be cutting himself out of almost every deal.

She stopped pushing at his side and John relaxed slightly. That had been more uncomfortable than he'd expected. The woman then pressed her ear against his shirtfront, instructing him to breathe.

She listened and she frowned. Then, finally, she sat back in her chair and looked at him.

"Are you married?" she asked. "Children?"

"Yes. I have a daughter; she's fourteen." John wasn't at all sure what this had to do with him feeling like his heart was exploding but it seemed to mean something to the woman because she was nodding thoughtfully.

"And you do not see her?"

"I see her," John snapped. It was true that he had missed her last birthday, but he sent her a very expensive ultralight computer. And, sure, he had not been able to come see the play she had been in this semester but Cherie was there, as were both sets of grandparents. His work gave her a big house to live in and a plush college fund, and that would serve her better than any single afternoon with her father.

"Not as often as you want to," the old woman amended and *that,* John could not argue. He missed his daughter just like he missed his wife. He saw them, these days, mostly through screens, large and small. But what could he do? He couldn't just stop working and there were no sick days or vacations for CEOs trying to build a company. All of this was for them, and if that meant being away from them, then so be it.

"Your liver is three times the size it should be," the old woman told him. "And your lungs are congested, which is probably related to the anxiety that you feel. I can give you herbal medicines that will help, just like your pills will help, but you must fix the real problem."

"The *real* problem?" John asked. "And what is that?"

The old woman smiled at him. For the first time, her face was gentle.

"You know the problem," she said, "and you know how to solve it. You are just afraid to do what must be done."

"I can't just abandon my responsibilities," John said. He felt an unaccountable anger swelling up inside him, almost as uncontrolled and alarming as the feeling of panic. "If I don't do this work, no one will."

"So you are alone," the old woman said, not reacting at all to the frustration in his voice.

"Yes!" he said, much louder and more tortured that he had expected. That, more than anything else, was what he dwelled upon when he thought about his attack. He was all alone in that hotel room, alone inside his own head and his own body, both of which had betrayed him. If he had died there, if his heart had leapt out of his chest, he would have died alone and no one would have known until an unlucky cleaning lady let herself in. There was such a weight to loneliness and a weight to his uncomplaining silence as well.

"There is no one to help me," he added, much more softly.

The woman shook her head.

"But you are here now. Someone helped you."

John thought of the woman at the front desk, her calm and steady voice on the phone and the way she had reached out to him later, finding some kinship with him. He thought of the energetic EMT assuring him that he was going to be OK. He thought about this old woman in front of him, how she had named him family and spoken to him frankly.

"There are people who will help you," she said. "But you have to find them. And you have to trust them when you do."

John thought about Cherie, about the stilted phone call he had with her in which he tried to avoid lying outright about his hospital trip. He could hear it in her voice, how she didn't believe him and how it hurt her, knowing that he was keeping something from her. When had his desire to protect her become something that stood between them like a concrete wall?

"Where is your home?" the woman asked, getting up and walking over to a small desk in the corner.

"Uh . . . Toronto," John managed. *Wherever Cherie is*, he thought, *wherever our girl is.*

"There is a naturopath in Toronto. I know her and she is very good. I will tell her about you and you will go see her. She can help you if you let her."

She had been flicking through an old-school Rolodex, but she looked up at him then and gave him a stern look. Again, he was reminded of his grandmother.

"And now," she said, "I think you should go home to your people."

John packed the old woman's careful herbal formulations—packaged neatly in plastic—in his suitcase, right next to his two-thirds-full bottle of prescription meds. On the plane, he switched out his usual scotch for a ginger ale, prompting the man next to him to ask him, "You in recovery?"

He looked at man, noticing his own innocuous can of Coke, and shook his head.

"I have . . . stomach troubles," John said lamely.

The man smiled at him a little sheepishly.

"Sorry, no offense intended. I'm usually pretty good at spotting other . . . members of the tribe, I guess you'd say."

John shook his head.

"No, that's . . . no offense at all."

The house was empty when he arrived, but John had expected that. It was 3:00 p.m. on a school day. In about forty-five minutes, Cherie would be coming home after having picked up their daughter at school, and that gave him enough time to make a few phone calls.

First, he called the naturopath whom the old woman had recommended and made an appointment for the following Wednesday.

Then, he phoned his therapist, whom he had stopped seeing about a year and a half ago, when he'd started the CEO job.

"Yes," he said, "I'd like to resume our sessions."

Then, he dug deep into the back of his closet and found the pair of running shoes he'd bought around that same time, intending to enter a marathon with Cherie. There was a thin layer of dust on the box but the shoes, themselves, still fit. They felt comfortable, even cradled his feet.

He was still trying them on when he heard the sound of a key in the front door, and he smiled. It was his family, his tribe, and they were coming to be with him.

www.kreat.ca

90-days to the life you desire

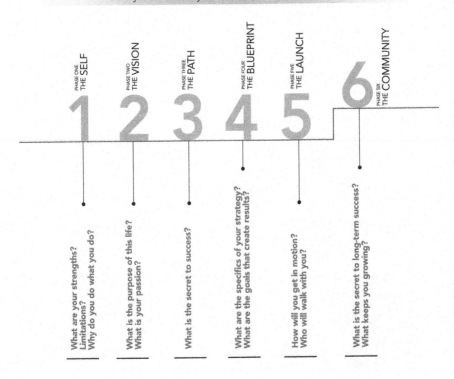

The Way of the Quiet Warrior™

COMPLETE this Self – Assessment Quiz then:
Visit www.kreat.ca to TAKE PROFILE and SCHEDULE a DISCOVERY LAB

THE SELF:

On a scale of 1 to 5 rate how well you know WHY you do what you do ☐ score
I consistently live my life with CLEAN MOTIVES ☐yes ☐no
I know my top 5 strengths and top 3 limitations ☐yes ☐no

THE VISION:

I have a written DMP Statement and have anchored it within myself ☐yes ☐no
I know my true purpose and burning desires ☐yes ☐no

THE PATH:

I consistently keep a positive mental attitude ☐yes ☐no
I have tools to think and feel like my highest self ☐yes ☐no

THE BLUEPRINT:

I have a written plan linked to my DMP Statement ☐yes ☐no
I know how to turn my blueprint into reality ☐yes ☐no

THE LAUNCH AND THE COMMUNITY:

I mastermind with 1 or more people regularly to manifest my DMP ☐yes ☐no

Success Feels Incredible. Happiness Can Last a Lifetime.

KRE-AT
PURPOSE | ACTION | LIFE

ABOUT THE
AUTHOR

 Tom is a senior business leader, speaker and published author with more than 30 years experience helping build and grow companies in Canada and the USA. Tom brings leadership experience from the Financial Services, IT, TELCO, Not-For-Profit, and Health sectors. His career includes senior roles in many of Canada's prestigious companies including President and CEO, and Chairman of the Board.

As Founder and CEO of KRE-AT™ Tom is the world's only motive based leadership expert. In concert with his business expertise, Tom's intense travel and study of the science behind success has enabled him to create a proven coaching and mentorship formula called The Way of the Quiet Warrior™. This dynamic program helps leaders manifest success by discovering purpose, taking action and living life their way.

Previously, Tom was General Manager with Ocean West Financial, Chief Operating Officer of the Annex Group, one of BC's fastest growing IT Professional Service firms. He was CEO with CRI Canada, a Division of AEGON - a supplier of software and financial services globally. At TELUS, one of Canada's largest telecommunications companies, Tom held a dual role of Director, Customer Excellence and Director, Enterprise Marketing. VanTel Credit Union was his first executive role as Vice President, Sales Marketing and Operations and previously he held Management roles with Toronto Dominion Bank.

Tom has served on a number of industry boards and serves as Chairman of the Board for MDABC working to pioneer a change in the Mental Health model. In his work with Mackay CEO Forums, Tom Chair's and mentors multiple CEO and Executive peer groups helping populate the world with better leaders.

Tom is married to his business partner, Anna, and together they have three children. Tom enjoys travel, experimenting with cooking and giving to help others achieve their life goals.

www.kreat.ca

A free eBook edition is available with the purchase of this book.

To claim your free eBook edition:

1. Download the Shelfie app.
2. Write your name in upper case in the box.
3. Use the Shelfie app to submit a photo.
4. Download your eBook to any device.

Shelfie

A free eBook edition is available
with the purchase of this print book.

CLEARLY PRINT YOUR NAME ABOVE IN UPPER CASE

Instructions to claim your free eBook edition:
1. Download the Shelfie app for Android or iOS
2. Write your name in **UPPER CASE** above
3. Use the Shelfie app to submit a photo
4. Download your eBook to any device

Print & Digital Together Forever.

Snap a photo Free eBook Read anywhere

The Morgan James
Speakers Group

Morgan James makes all of our titles available
through the Library for All Charity Organizations.

www.LibraryForAll.org

CPSIA information can be obtained
at www.ICGtesting.com
Printed in the USA
BVOW08s0220190517
484354BV00001B/2/P